ON STAGE WITH ELVIS PRESLEY

The backstage stories of Elvis' legendary TCB Band

JAMES BURTON • RON TUTT • GLEN D. HARDIN • JERRY SCHEFF

and Music Director, Joe Guercio

As told to
Stuart Coupe

Foreword by
Jerry Schilling

SEG Publishing
468 N. Camden Drive
Suite 200
Beverly Hills, CA 90210

On Stage with Elvis Presley

Edition 003 @ 2020
Printed in the United States of America

ISBN 978-0-578-77746-7
www.stigedgren.com

A NOTE FROM THE PUBLISHER

In the spring of 1997, I was sitting in my hotel room in Nashville nursing a broken leg with crutches and exhausted after a long day of rehearsals with Donna Summer. The phone rang and it was Todd Morgan from Graceland - a call that literally changed my life.

He went on to describe a "vision" he had for a new Elvis Presley 'live' concert for the 20th Anniversary of his passing - essentially putting Elvis back 'on stage', via video, playing together with his original bandmates, background singers and orchestra. Todd asked me if I was interested in producing the show – of course, the answer was yes (duh).

We worked together a few years earlier on a show called *Elvis–The Tribute*, my first 'EP' project and introduction to the amazing folks at Elvis Presley Enterprises.

Todd was interested in the Live Video I created for Natalie Cole singing 'Unforgettable' with her late father, Nat King Cole, and asked if we could apply this concept to Elvis. The technology was brand new and took weeks to match-up ONE song, so the thought of producing a full length 2-hour concert for the greatest superstar to ever perform on stage was daunting – and super exciting.

We put together an A-Team made up of Randy Johnson as Director and Joe Guercio as Musical Director. We would all brainstorm at Graceland trying to come up with the 'Ultimate' EP Concert. The mindset was simple, and yet complex - how to produce a show for Elvis Presley if he was alive - a massive responsibility - and a tremendous honor.

One of the unknowns was the TCB Band - this being the first time they agreed to play together since Elvis' death - for one reason or another, it had been 20 years, and that was the goal, to win them over and bring this idea to life - like bringing together all the King's Men.

During the first rehearsal and soundcheck at the Mid-South Coliseum, with everyone together, Elvis on the giant screen singing with the TCB Band, The Sweet Inspirations, The Stamps and Imperials - I'll never forget hearing the sound in the arena for the first time and running towards the stage yelling "That's' IT, That's IT!" - it was the most incredible experience hearing Elvis "live" back in the building! And the SOUND - standing on stage and hearing the TCB Band play together brought one word to mind, THUNDER. I instantly understood why Elvis appreciated them so much.

One of the worst decisions I've ever made as a young Lighting Designer finishing up my first show at The Las Vegas Hilton with Dionne Warwick and was invited by the staff to stay for the next night's opening of 'EP' – the decision not to stay and see him perform still haunts me – especially, because one year later, Elvis was gone.

Even though I never saw him perform live, I've had a very special relationship with him through video – hundreds of hours of raw footage from the 'That's The Way It Is' performances at The Las Vegas Hilton, the Aloha satellite concert, and Elvis On Tour. In a dark editing studio, I became consumed with how amazing this performer really was – his natural moves and magnetism – not to mention the best looking guy on the planet.

After working with some of the finest performers in history, including Michael Jackson, Frank Sinatra and Barbra Streisand – who are superb – Elvis remains a notch above any artist – in a league of his own.

The TCB Band is legendary – I idolized them in my early career, and still do. Thank you, James & Louise, – thank you Ronnie & Donna – thank you Glen & Betty – thank you Jerry – and deepest thanks to one of my favorite people ever in life, Joe Guercio. It's been a privilege to work with all of you and know you and your families. I'll always treasure our collaboration and friendship.

My sincere thanks to Priscilla Presley, Lisa-Marie Presley, Jack Soden, Gary Hovey, Debbie Johnson, Regina Gambill, Angie Marchese, Jen Swearingen, Bevin Baddorf and a host of other wonderful EPE/Graceland colleagues over the years – and especially to the late Todd Morgan, who had the 'seed' of an idea that would change the way live events are presented.

Please enjoy these wonderful stories – it took 20 years to publish this manuscript - not sure what took so long :)

Stig Edgren
Co-Creator/Producer 'Elvis-In Concert'
Los Angeles, 2020

Every great rock and roll singer needs a great rock and roll band, and Elvis has got one. James Burton, the guitarist, can pick Sun era rockabilly, country twang, laid-back bluesy fills and sharp, singing single string leads. Bassist Jerry Scheff and drummer Ronnie Tutt are super tight; when they mail down the beat, it stays nailed down. Pianist Glen D. Hardin knows when to honk and when to tonk.

BOB PALMER, Rolling Stone, 1972

If love truly is going out of fashion forever, which I do not believe, then along with our nurtured indifference to each other will be an even more contemptuous indifference to each other's object of reverence . . . But I can guarantee you one thing: we will never again agree on anything as we agreed on Elvis.

LESTER BANGS - Where Were You When Elvis Died?

On the stage itself, Presley surrounds himself with the best that money can buy. Tutt is the only true big-band rock drummer I have ever seen in action and he is magnificent. But then too, it isn't everyone who has James Burton himself for a lead guitarist and the Sweet Inspirations for a third of the background voices."

JON LANDAU - In Praise of Elvis Presley

This book is dedicated to the finest entertainer in the history of live musical performance - Elvis Presley

TABLE OF CONTENTS

INTRODUCTION
THE ONCE AND FUTURE KING

There was no mistaking the content of the Email. The producer of Elvis - The Concert was looking for an Australian journalist to travel with the group on their upcoming tour of Australia. Was I interested? Did I have the time? I thought about it for all of three seconds before responding in the affirmative. Only a complete fool would pass up the opportunity to spend three weeks travelling with the T.C.B. Band, The Sweet Inspirations, The Imperials, Joe Guercio and the other people in the touring organization. I emailed Stig Edgren telling him I'd been an Elvis fan all of my life, had heard every record, read the majority of books written about the singer and visited Graceland twice. He was convinced.

As a result, I spent the majority of November 1999 travelling to Brisbane, Adelaide, Sydney and Melbourne watching Elvis - The Concert, talking with the participants and recording their recollections of being an essential part of the Elvis Presley experience from 1969 until 1977. I flew with the tour party, stayed in the same hotels, watched rehearsals, saw the show every night, spent some of the most enjoyable nights of my life in various bars after shows and, along the way, made some new friends. It wasn't completely perfect however - try as I did, I couldn't convince the organizers to take me on the Japanese leg of the tour on route back to the States. Maybe next time.

To be honest, whilst I was overwhelmed by the opportunity to spend a considerable amount of time with some of my musical idols, there was a degree of cynicism around me prior to the tour. What, you're going to spend three weeks watching a dead person on a big video screen with old people playing along, was a fairly typical response from my friends. For me there was a mixture of excitement coupled with a real feeling that this was just toooo bizarre for words. I kidded with my friends that I'd probably see the first show or two and then spend the rest of tour checking out the bars nearby and finding the best place to eat dinner. Like the show was going to be different each night. Elvis wasn't really in a position to improvise, was he?

That cynicism totally disappeared after watching a long, long five-hour rehearsal in Adelaide and seeing the first concert the night after. I was floored and spent the two hours of Elvis - The Concert brushing away tears and with chills running down my spine. In the space of two hours I became a one-person publicist for the show, calling everyone I knew around the country spluttering words like - I know you think I'm crazy, but you MUST see this show. It is AMAZING!

As any fan knows Elvis never performed outside of the United States. Apparently, there were offers to come to Australia during the 1970s but as with similar offers from other countries, nothing ever happened. With the exception of the handful of Australians who'd made the pilgrimage to the States to see a show, my experience of Elvis was limited to records, CDs, and videos. And to be equally candid my real love was Elvis' 50s recordings. Prior to seeing Elvis - The Concert I had a studied appreciation for his 70's material but it was simply that - studied. I sensed that it was much greater than I was giving it credit for but something about the public perception of the last decade of Elvis' life clouded a real appreciation for what was being created during this time.

The media told me that the 70's was an era of fat Elvis, drugged Elvis, uncaring Elvis, crazy Elvis. Naively, that stopped me from really listening to the astonishing power and intensity in his voice, and the truly awesome interaction between Elvis and the musicians and singers who had been assembled to perform with him.

Night after night of the Australian tour (I didn't miss a second of any show) I sat riveted as the giant screens showed Elvis at the pinnacle of his creativity, whilst below him some of the finest musicians and singers imaginable re-created the intensity of a live Elvis concert. Needless to say, I wasn't the only one enraptured. Initially I'd wondered about the audience drawing power of a show like Elvis - The Concert. I knew it had done extremely well in the States and Europe, but weren't Australian's going to feel like it was a cheap shot at dragging hard earned money out of their pockets? Those thoughts could only have come from a mind that was temporarily blinded to the enduring attraction of Elvis' music. Every show was a sell-out with between 12,000 and 15,000 people screaming, dancing and being emotionally moved by what they were experiencing. People rushed to the stage to try and touch the musicians and the audience, as if in choir, sang along with every song.

I had imagined that the people who'd turn out for Elvis - The Concert would all be old folks. Wrong again! The old cliché of suitable for ages eight to 80 was absolutely true. Frequently it was a case where three generations of families were sitting together. There were punks, fifties music fans, young children and every other imaginable cultural demographic assembled together for just one reason - to celebrate the life and music of Elvis Presley.

To compile the stories in this book, I spent extended periods with each of the participants during the course of the Australian tour. Finally, after everyone had told their stories in isolation, we gathered for a riotous four hour lunch in Sydney where everyone compared notes and cleared up differing recollections of events, many of which happened at a time when none of the participants had the slightest idea that they'd be of interest to other people many decades later.

This book is not meant to be a chronological look at Elvis Presley's career during the 70s. For that detail and insight, I'd recommended Peter Guralnick's magnificent Careless Love or Jerry Hopkins' racier but equally insightful Elvis: The Final Years.

Another thing that everyone agreed on is that this is most definitely not a mud racking, scandal-spilling book. The T.C.B. Band members know that there are more than enough books of that nature available and were determined that they present the positive side of Elvis. If you're looking for terrific inside stories about life with Elvis, then keep reading - but if all you're interested in is the sex and drugs side of Elvis then there's plenty of other books for you to read. This simply ain't one of them, okay.

This book is the recollections and impressions of James Burton, Ronnie Tutt, Jerry Scheff, Glen D. Hardin and Joe Guercio. As much as possible I've let them tell the stories, and only provided a bit of scaffolding to assist in the structure and flow of their recollections.

Ultimately this book provides an intimate look into the behind the scene world of touring and recording with Elvis, a story about the man behind the performer, a story that hasn't been told.

When Elvis - The Concert tour kicked-off, and the interview process began, and all the misconception about what I was experiencing had melted with the ice in my glass, a friend quipped to me - Hey, this is probably the one book about Elvis that hasn't been written - but should be written. And I think she was right.

Stuart Coupe

Sydney, Australia, April 2000

FOREWORD

When I first became friends with Elvis in 1954, his musical career was just beginning, and he was playing with a band that had come together at Sam Phillips' Sun Studios: guitarist Scotty Moore, bassist Bill Black, and later, drummer D.J. Fontana. It was with those great players that Elvis found his sound and cut early hits such as "That's All Right," Hound Dog," and Heartbreak Hotel." The first time I saw Elvis perform live was at the Ellis Auditorium in Memphis in February of 1955. Promoters had been billing Elvis as "The Hillbilly Cat," but to me, Elvis—spurred on by Scotty and Bill's musical support—prowled the stage like a hungry tiger.

I was too young to go on the road with that band, and when I went to work for Elvis ten years later, he had stopped doing concert performances to focus on his movie career. I was more than happy to be a part of his world, but I figured I had missed out on the excitement of touring with him. Elvis was always looking for artistic challenges, though, and in 1969 he decided that it was time to put a band together and get back up on stage.

He had just done some of his finest studio recordings and had hits like "Suspicious Minds" and "In the Ghetto" on the radio, so any of the top studio session players in LA or Memphis would have jumped at the chance to be in Elvis's band. But he didn't want a band made up of the 'usual suspect' session guys. He wanted 'his guys'—players that had the feel and passion to give him the musical launch pad he needed to do the kind of show he wanted to do.

Elvis's first call was to James Burton, the ace guitarist who'd been part of the house band for TV's "Shindig," and who had played with talents ranging from Ricky Nelson to Frank Sinatra. Elvis wanted James' guitar to be an anchor of his band's sound, and he also wanted James to help him with auditions for the rest of the players. I was there at the RCA studio in Hollywood when those auditions took place, and it was incredible to watch the level of excitement Elvis had as he worked with so many great musicians, trying to find the perfect match. After years of slickly recorded movie soundtrack albums, Elvis now wanted a band that would surprise people. He wanted a band that would kick ass.

He knew that the key to the band's sound would be in the rhythm section. I remember that whenever he and the Memphis Mafia went out to see other bands play, he'd say to me "Watch the bass player—he's always the coolest guy on stage." At the auditions, he decided that the cool guy he wanted on stage with him was Jerry Scheff. Jerry had a reputation as an inventive, tasteful player, whose basslines had anchored pop hits by the Association, Bobby Sherman, and the Monkees. But at the auditions he was encouraged to cut loose, and he won a spot in the band playing what Elvis described as "thundering" bass (Jerry later added that thunder to the Doors "LA Woman" album).

For a drummer, Elvis made his most surprising pick. He had heard all the top session players, but there was one last guy who he wanted to audition—a drummer named Ronnie Tutt who didn't have that many pro credits, and who rolled up to the RCA studio in a station wagon packed with his family and all his earthly belongings. Elvis told Ronnie they were going to run through a couple of tunes, and he wanted Ronnie to use the drums to accentuate his moves as he sang. They started a song, and Elvis kept calling out more directions to Ronnie, telling him to follow the moves and hit the accents harder. Ronnie started looking like he was playing angry, and the whole band's energy started to jump. Afterwards, Elvis said, "I need somebody on stage who plays with my temperament. And the guy with the beard's got it." Ronnie was in.

Glen D. Hardin joined the TCB band as an excellent piano player, but as an arranger he became one of the band's greatest secret weapons. Somebody had to figure out what all those great players on stage were actually going to play, and that was Glen. I remember late nights after shows when we'd all be partying up in Elvis's suite, and Glen wouldn't be around because he was off somewhere working like crazy to come up with arrangements for songs Elvis wanted to play the next night. Glen liked to party as much as the rest of us, but he was also a consummate professional.

When Elvis began performing again, he was backed by the TCB band, an orchestra led by 'Maestro' Joe Guercio, and Elvis's hand-picked groups of back-up singers—the Imperials (later the Stamps) and the Sweet Inspirations (I was such a fan of the Sweets that I married one of them—Myrna Smith). These days, top acts from every genre play in Las Vegas, but I think it's important to note that Elvis and the TCB band changed music history by being the first act to bring the sounds of vital rock 'n' roll to the city.

I was there for the opening weekend of shows at the International Hotel in 1969, and from the first notes Elvis sang I realized how much I'd missed watching him do what he could do on a concert stage. This was his room, his show, his music—his band. That hungry tiger I'd seen at the Ellis Auditorium was back—strong and ferocious as ever.

The excitement of Elvis shows lives on through Stig Edgren's "Elvis: In Concert" productions. Beginning in Memphis with a commemoration of the 20th anniversary of Elvis's death, Stig was able to re-create the atmosphere of original concerts by bringing back together TCB band members, singers and conductor Guercio to accompany Elvis performances captured in amazing archival film footage.

Since then, "Elvis: In Concert" has toured around the world to sold-out crowds. I've had the pleasure of being a part of many those tours, and in 2019, Priscilla Presley and I hosted a show at London's O2 Arena that teamed the TCB band with the Royal Philharmonic Orchestra. The audience reaction to these shows always feels as passionate as the way audiences reacted when Elvis was still with us, and that makes it a very emotional experience for all of us on stage.

I remember the moments before many of Elvis's shows, when the "Theme to 2001" would start playing and he and I would engage in some dynamic karate resistance moves—his way of getting physically pumped up so that when Ronnie Tutt began his powerful drum intro, Elvis could take the stage bigger than life.

Elvis was an artist, and the concert stage was his greatest medium. He wanted to deliver a peak performance on that stage, and the TCB band was made of players he personally selected to get him to that level.

As usual, when Elvis was allowed to make his own decisions about his music, he made the right ones. He wanted James, Glen, Jerry and Ronnie behind him, and the sound of all that talent coming together, and still taking care of business like no one else.

Jerry Schilling
Los Angeles, 2020

CHAPTER 1

"LADIES AND GENTLEMEN, I'D LIKE TO INTRODUCE YOU TO THE MEMBERS OF MY BAND . . . "

Chapter One

"ON THE GUITAR, MR JAMES BURTON"

James Burton began his career at age 14, playing guitar in the house band for Shreveport's famed Louisiana Hayride. While playing in Dale Hawkins' band in 1955, he wrote the music for the hit song Susie-Q and recorded it with Hawkins. In 1957, he began a nine-year run as guitarist for Ricky Nelson, including recording sessions and concert tours with Nelson and weekly appearances on the Nelson family's classic television show The Adventures of Ozzie and Harriet. By the mid-sixties, Burton was in demand as a session player and made some recordings of his own. Among the many artists he has recorded with over the years are: Elvis Presley, Ricky Nelson, Jerry Lee Lewis, Roy Orbison, John Denver, Johnny Cash, George Harrison, Rosanne Cash, Frank Sinatra, Henry Mancini, The Byrds, The Everly Brothers, Tina Turner, Elvis Costello, Andy Williams. Dolly Parton, Linda Ronstadt, Hank Williams. Jr., Emmylou Harris, Willie Nelson, Dean Martin, Glen Campbell, Merle Haggard, Waylon Jennings, Arlo Guthrie, Johnny Mathis, The Mamas and the Papas, The Mills Brothers, Herb Alpert, and many others.

Elvis himself called James Burton and asked him to put together a band for his 1969 engagement in Las Vegas. Burton was Elvis' lead guitarist in concerts for Vegas and national tours, and on many recordings, from 1969 until Elvis' death in 1977. The next long-term gig for Burton was recording and touring with John Denver for a number of years. Today, he continues to work with a wide variety of artists in the studio and on the road, and he is involved in a broad range of projects. Among guitarists James Burton has become an icon, and his influence on generations of guitar players, both the famous and the unknown, is unmistakable. He was inducted in the Rock'n Roll Hall Of Fame and voted #19 of all-time greatest guitar players.

"ON THE DRUMS, MR RONNIE TUTT."

Ronnie Tutt is originally from Dallas, Texas. He studied music at the University of North Texas, played gigs in the Dallas/Fort Worth area, and held staff positions (drums and vocals) at two "jingle" studios. In 1963 he moved to Memphis and played with some of that city's great rhythm sections during an exciting time in Memphis music history. In 1969 he auditioned for Elvis, who was putting together a band for his Las Vegas engagement. He got the job. Beyond talented as a drummer, what seemed to put him above the competition was his way of connecting with Elvis - watching him, making eye contact, anticipating where Elvis was going with a song. Their "musical communication" was a key part of making a great show. From 1969 to 1977 he was Elvis' drummer on stage and on a number of recordings, for a long time Ronnie Tutt was a studio musician in Los Angeles, later relocating to Nashville. For several years he was part of the Jerry Garcia Band, doing albums and extensive touring. Since 1981 he has been a member of the Neil Diamond Band, recording and touring around the world. Tutt is endorsed by DW Drums, Paiste Cymbals and Calato/Regal Tip drumsticks.

"PLAYING THE PIANO, MR GLEN D. HARDIN."

Glen D. Hardin grew up in Texas and made his way to Los Angeles in the fall of 1961 after leaving the U.S. Navy. By early 1962 he was playing piano at the Palomino Club and soon started touring with the Crickets. Over the years he has worked as an arranger and recording session pianist with artists such as Elvis Presley, Emmylou Harris, John Denver, Merle Haggard, Marty Robbins, George Jones, Dolly Parton, Tanya Tucker, The Everly Brothers, Ricky Nelson, Travis Tritt, Trisha Yearwood, Alan Jackson, Vince Gill, Willie Nelson, Kenny Rogers & The First Edition, Bing Crosby, Andy Williams, Jim Nabors. Dean Martin,

Sammy Davis Jnr., Sonny & Cher, k.d. lang, Roy Orbison, Linda Ronstadt, Ike & Tina Turner, Cass Elliot, Ricky Skaggs, Marty Stuart, Tammy Wynette and many others. He toured with Emmylou Harris for three years, the Crickets for eleven, and John Denver for sixteen. His work with Elvis was from 1970 to 1976, playing live concerts with Elvis, creating some of his arrangements and being a part of numerous Elvis recordings.

"ON THE BASS, MR JERRY SCHEFF."

Jerry Scheff grew up in the San Francisco Bay area, started playing tuba in grammar school and, by seventh grade, got into playing string bass. His musical bent was towards jazz and R&B. By age fifteen he was playing in clubs in his new hometown of Sacramento and back in San Francisco. As a high school senior Scheff joined the U.S. Navy and wound up in the Navy's school of music in Washington, D.C. taking a nine-month course studying theory and harmony and getting to play with some great musicians. After the course ended, he stayed on to teach, moonlighting as a player in jazz clubs, then the Navy transferred him to San Diego. Sometime after his service discharge Scheff moved to Los Angeles and played regularly at a club called The Sands in Watts, where a teen-aged Billy Preston often appeared doing James Brown covers. Oddly enough, bass players Scheff began his work in the L.A. recording session scene playing valve trombone. The first hit records Scheff played bass on was an album by the group The Association, including the singles Along Comes Mary and Cherish. On Mary Scheff made a bass mistake that got left in, so the thrill of hearing his work on a radio hit was counterbalanced by his cringing every time he heard the mistake. However, a couple of years later, it was gratifying to hear an "elevator music" cover of it that had the bass player copying Scheff's part, bad note and all. A special career highlight was playing on The Doors' album LA Woman.

Over the years Scheff recorded with Bobby Sherman, Tiny Tim, Johnny Mathis, Nancy Sinatra, Sammy Davis, Jr., Bobby Vinton, The Everly Brothers, the Nitty Gritty Dirt Band, Dionne

Warwick, Barbra Streisand, Linda Ronstadt, Judy Collins and many others. By the late sixties he crossed paths with guitarist James Burton, who remembered Scheff's work and called him when putting together the band for Elvis in 1969. Scheff worked with Elvis from 1969 to 1973 and 1975 to 1977, on stage and on a number of recordings. Reflecting on those years, Scheff says "Elvis had a big impact on my career. It was like going to school." Today, he continues to work as a session musician with a wide array of artists. A passion in recent years has been song writing. Although much of his career has been working with rock and pop greats, he still enjoys sitting in to play a little jazz every once in a while, as he says, "to keep the cobwebs clear." Both of Scheff's sons, Darin and Jason, are musicians. Jason Scheff took over Peter Cetera's spot in the band Chicago.

"AND MY MUSICAL DIRECTOR, MR JOE GUERCIO."

Joe Guercio has enjoyed a prolific career, but he is probably best known and admired for his work with Elvis Presley. He was musical director and conductor for Elvis' concert shows from the summer of 1970 to August 1977 when Elvis made his last concert appearance. Elvis was known for spontaneity and improvisation on stage and the cast had to be ready for anything. Guercio remembers "He'd just turn around and start a tune. The rhythm section knew him backwards and forwards, but when you're up there conducting a twenty-six-piece orchestra, what are you going to do?" Guercio was musical director for the International Hilton in Las Vegas when the work with Elvis began. Along with the obvious contributions he made to Elvis' shows, including many of the triumphs of Elvis' "concert era", it was Joe Guercio who created the now almost iconic six-note theme for Elvis' stage entrances and bows. It was also Guercio who suggested that Elvis' shows open with the Theme from 2001 - A Space Odyssey (Also Sprach Zarathustra). The inspiration came when Guercio and his late wife saw the now-classic science fiction movie in a theatre, for when the music began Mrs. Guercio whispered to her husband "You'd think Elvis was about to enter."

Joe Guercio first left his native Buffalo, NY as an accompanist for Patti Paige. He has lived in Las Vegas since 1967 and has been a musical director for Diana Ross, Jim Nabors, Florence Henderson, Diahann Carroll, and Steve Lawrence and Eddie Gorme, among others. His arrangement of the medley Sweet Inspiration/ Where You Lead was a 1972 hit for Barbra Streisand, and his arrangement of The Way We were/ Try To remember was a 1975 hit for Gladys Knight. Guercio's work with Natalie Cole to reunite her on stage in duet with her late father, Nat King Cole, pre-dated her famous early 1990's duet recordings and videos with Mr. Cole. Guercio accompanied blues legend B.B. King to Rome to meet Pope John Paul 11 and perform in the Vatican's fifth Christmas concert. Joe Guercio served as musical director for the Elvis in Concert '97 event in Memphis and reprises this role in the touring production Elvis - The Concert.

CHAPTER 2

FOLLOW THAT DREAM

Chapter Two

Ronnie Tutt still remembers the night Elvis told him about a dream he'd had. It occurred sometime soon after the successful '68 Comeback Concert when Colonel Tom Parker was trying to work out how best to build on the impact of that television special. The Colonel knew one thing for sure - that he wanted Elvis to perform a season at the Las Vegas Hilton. But not being the most creative of individuals, the Colonel had pretty much decided that Elvis perform a show that was a slight extension of the Comeback Concert. In other words, it would be an extension of the movies Elvis had made, combined with an array of dancers and a predictable song selection. The reality would be a stage version of the bland films that had stunted Elvis' career for the previous decade.

At the time Las Vegas wasn't known for full blown rock in roll concerts, but for an endless parade of glitzy showbiz performers, the majority of them way past their creative peaks. The Colonel really wanted Elvis to follow this path. It was safe - and the money was good. Very good.

Elvis, however, was not enthusiastic about these plans. He'd had a taste of live performance with the Comeback Concert and was itching to continue performing - but something just wasn't right about what the Colonel had in mind. He was, to say the least, uncomfortable with the Vegas idea but couldn't come up with a better idea than what was being pushed towards him.

"Elvis told me that one night he woke in the middle of the night and he'd had a dream," recalls Ronnie.

"He said in my dream I saw myself onstage. I saw myself standing in front of a hard, driving rock band that was really kicking. On one side I saw a white male gospel quartet and on the other side I saw a black female soul group, and then I saw this big orchestra as the background to it, and we were doing a live concert."

Elvis was so excited about the dream that he did something he never did. He got on the phone in the middle of the night and called Colonel Parker, waking him up. Elvis told the Colonel about his dream in a voice that resembled a young, excited kid. The Colonel was not at all impressed by Elvis' idea and told him as much.

As Ronnie recalls from talking with Elvis, "Elvis told him, 'I'll tell you what Colonel, out of all due respect, we're just going to do it this way or we're not going to do it at all' and then he hung up on the Colonel. He said that it was the only time in his life he had confronted the Colonel in this manner. They'd had disagreements before, but this time Elvis took a really firm stand. And thank God he did because it worked out extremely well. Otherwise it would have been another Vegas musical. Just having Elvis there would have still meant it was great, but it wouldn't have been any more than some of those production numbers from his movies."

CHAPTER 3

A BAND TO TAKE CARE OF BUSINESS

Chapter Three

With the Colonel convinced - or at least begrudgingly agreeing to go along with Elvis' wishes - it came down to the logistics of putting together a band and knocking the show into shape.

The first person called to be involved in that was guitarist James Burton who had originally been asked to perform with Elvis at the '68 Comeback Concert.

Unfortunately, James was not available for that show and recommended a friend of his. Why was James unavailable to play with Elvis at the time? He probably had one of the best excuses. He had just been booked by Frank Sinatra for an album he was doing with producer Jimmy Bowen.

Come 1969 and as Elvis prepared for more live work and the first Las Vegas season, James received a call at home. Initially however he didn't feel like talking as he was snowed under with seemingly endless session work.

"I was in the shower getting ready to go to work", James recalls. "I was very busy with studio work, doing five or six sessions a day, seven days a week. It was an unbelievable time. My wife came in and said you have a phone call from a Mr. Joe Esposito. That name didn't ring a bell so I said to my wife ask him if I can call him back, and my wife said well, I think maybe you should take this call. So, I went in and got on the phone and Joe Esposito said, 'Hi James, very nice to talk to you. I'm Joe Esposito and I have someone here who'd like to speak with you.'

"Elvis got on the phone. Oh man. We started talking and Elvis was very gentlemanly and told me how he'd followed my entire career and watched me on television on the Ozzie and Harriett Show with Ricky (Nelson). He said I watched the Ozzie and Harriett Show just to watch you play guitar at the end of the show. I thought that was pretty interesting coming from the King of Rock'n Roll.

"When Elvis called, we talked for about three hours, and he asked me to put a band together. He said he was tired of doing movies and he wanted to get back into doing rock shows for a live audience, and that was where his heart was at. That is where he wanted to be.

"My telephone conversation with Elvis was quite interesting. It appeared that he had been listening to me for a while. It was through the Ricky Nelson records, but also, he'd heard about me from some people that worked with him. His record producer, Felton Jarvis, said that he had recommended me very highly to Elvis. And of course, Red West was taking credit for it. And then Charlie Hodge said that it was his idea. Elvis said later, all you guys are wrong, but I've always assumed that Felton Jarvis played a big part in it"

Whilst James had never met Elvis until they came together in 1969, the two had pursued not dissimilar musical paths. Elvis was obviously the best known figure in popular music at the time, but in the field of guitar playing James had a similar reputation, albeit one that wasn't as publicly acknowledged. Musicians however knew that James was as good as guitar players got.

"Back in the really early days I knew Scotty (Moore) and D.J. (Fontana) who is from my hometown of Shreveport, Louisiana. It was strange that Elvis and I didn't meet earlier because I was on the Louisiana Hayride when I was 14 years old playing guitar with the staff band playing behind George Jones, Johnny Horton and a whole bunch of other country artists.

"Then there was a chance that we could have met when I was playing guitar with Bob Luman, James recalls. Bob was a pretty good guitar player and did a lot of rockabilly. We did tours with Gene Vincent and The Blue Caps. Eddie Cochran and I used to go motorcycle riding together. It was Eddie, me, Gene and Ricky (Nelson) riding motorcycles together. But for whatever reason I didn't meet Elvis until 1969 even though I knew all the Memphis Mafia. I knew Red West, Sonny and all those guys. As a matter of fact, I was offered a job with Elvis when I was working with Ricky. Red West asked me in the '60s if I'd be interested in working with Elvis right after he got out of the army. I told Red that I was very happy playing with Ricky and that I didn't have a real good reason to change.

"Bob Luman actually did a lot of Elvis's songs because I played guitar like Scotty did. It was interesting the sound that Scotty got, the way he used an echo amp. I had no idea how he was getting that sound, but I found out later. We were playing a club one night in Louisiana with Bob, and Elvis's boys showed up - Scotty, D.J. and Bill (Black). They all came into this club and we asked them if they'd like to get up and play. Scotty got up onstage, but he wouldn't play any solos on Elvis tunes even though Bob did a lot of them. That seemed pretty strange to me. He'd played on all these records, but he was making me play the solos. When we took a break, Scotty told me he'd be right back. He went out to his car and bought in his amp and that was how he got that sound, using the echo amp. I thought that was pretty interesting because I was doing it all with my fingers. I'd learnt to play that way with my fingers but with Scotty I realized that his amp was doing all the work"

Still, when they finally found themselves in the same room, like all of the musicians who were to become members of the T.C.B. Band, James clicked with Elvis from the moment they first met.

"When we shook hands, it was like we'd known each other our whole lives and we'd worked together our whole lives." James says.

"He had so much charisma. He was just a Southern gentleman in his background and in his love for his parents and his love for his fellow man and the people who worked with him. He really appreciated the people there and he was just very, very relaxed and great to work with and be with"

Why Elvis wanted a new band in 1969 as opposed to sticking with Scotty Moore, Bill Black, D.J. Fontana and others who played with him on the '68 Comeback Concert is something that's never been explained. James suggests that it may have had something to do with the financial side of things, and that the older musicians wanted more for touring than either Elvis or, in particular, the Colonel, were prepared to pay.

Asked about his recollection of the events at the time, Ronnie says that he's not sure whether the decision to use a different band may have been financially driven.

"I did hear a rumor that the reasons the Jordanaires didn't do the shows and the Imperials did, was that the Jordanaires wanted an arm and a leg to play in Las Vegas. They apparently wanted a tremendous amount of money to do it. I don't know for sure if that's true, but that's the only thing that makes sense to me, particularly knowing Elvis propensity for hanging out and performing with the people he feels comfortable with. The musicians and singers he worked with were like family to him, so there must have been very strong reasons why he didn't use the people he'd worked with before"

Adding to the possible reasons behind Elvis' decision to work with the T.C.B. Band is something Ronnie observed from talking with Elvis over their time together.

"I think he was embarrassed about the music he did back in the early days, particularly the stuff for all the movies, but including the Sun material," he says.

"By the time we met him he'd become a totally different man. He became a self-educated man. You'd go into his bedroom and there were stacks of books around his walls. I really feel he was embarrassed about those early days. A lot of people say that his music was the most pure and wonderful music, but to him that was the most embarrassing time of his life. He didn't want to do it anymore and had become a totally different man. That earlier era was an embarrassment to him"

Joe adds: "His musical high was when he got everything together with the T.C.B. Band. That was his high. Everybody carries on about the guys before and, make no mistake, they were good players, but if any fan really thinks those guys could do what the T.C.B. Band did then they're very wrong. No way in the world. That's nothing against those dudes but they were coming off the back of a truck and the T.C.B. Band wasn't. This was a different kind of showbiz"

James: "That was part of the conversation when he called me in '69. He said to me, I'm sick of doing movies. I've told the Colonel I'm not doing another movie. He'd had nine years solid of movies. That's all he did in that time. He wanted to go back to doing live performances. He wanted a live audience"

Elvis met with James in Los Angeles and the work of putting the band together began almost immediately. As James remembers the genesis of the T.C.B. Band:

Jerry Scheff and I had worked together on many sessions. "We'd done several projects and I just love the way Jerry plays. He had that little bite that you get when you pop the strings. He was just a wonderful player, so I definitely had him on the top of my list"

For Jerry playing with Elvis in Las Vegas wasn't necessarily something he was particularly keen on doing. His background in music was very different from Elvis' but he couldn't help but be curious.

"James called up and said he was putting together a band for Elvis, so I thought I'd just go down and check it out, Jerry remembers. I was thinking that I probably wasn't going to do it, but I wanted to see what was going on. Anyway, I went down and did it and then I went home and told my wife you've got to come down tomorrow and hear this. She thought I was kidding but she came down the next day. Being there made me feel like I was going to school. It really opened up my mind to things other than my usual narrow scope. All the players were great, but I hadn't played that type of music before at all.

"At the rehearsal Larry Muhoberac was there with James. I was the only bass player. I asked James about it later and he said they never auditioned anyone else. So, I guess when he said we'll get Jerry Scheff, then that was cool"

Jerry had played trumpet on the soundtrack to an Elvis movie. As with James, who'd played on movie tracks for Viva Las Vegas and Girls Girls Girls, it was just something session players did at the time. It was simply a gig and they didn't think too much about who they were playing with.

"I think it was around 1966 and I was working with Billy Preston in Watts three nights a week, he recalls. I wasn't making very much money. Then Red West called me up and said, "are you Jerry Scheff, the trumpet player?", and I said yep. Actually, I played tuba, but I thought, what the heck. He told me that they were doing an Elvis Presley movie and wanted a five-piece horn section, so I said that is me. I borrowed this old silver trumpet which didn't even have a case and took it down there. I didn't play anything over a middle C for two days, collected my money and went home"

Jerry also apparently played bass on another Elvis movie. He doesn't recall the session at all, but a friend has subsequently told him that he was on the union contract.

"Obviously, I was so out of it that I didn't remember doing it," he laughs.

For Jerry, actually meeting Elvis wasn't that big a deal. He'd met a lot of music stars and legends before, and on top of that he wasn't a fan of Elvis. For him it was simply another audition for a job that he was far from convinced that he actually wanted or needed.

"I remember thinking he was a good-looking guy; Jerry says matter-of-factly about their first encounter. He wasn't dressed real flashy. I wasn't in awe of him at all. For me it was like okay he's a good-looking guy, but let's play and see what's going on. Elvis was a natural entertainer. He liked to entertain everybody. We'd be rehearsing and he'd do songs that we loved, especially in the first few days. He did things that he thought we would like, and we'd play em and it was fun. But then, say, two ladies would walk into the room and all of a sudden, he'd be into the love songs, literally. Whoever was there he'd play for them. He wanted everyone to enjoy what he was doing so he would divide it up and do something for everybody"

When Jerry's wife came to a rehearsal she too fell under Elvis' spell.

"Of course, like everyone other woman she thought he was so good looking," Jerry laughs.

"The thing that she liked about him, and that I liked about him as well, and the reason I continued to like him, was that he was a natural, pure singer. It was the same thing that Frank Sinatra had. There are people like Bruce Springsteen and Garth Brooks who are entertainers in the sense that they're thinking about how they look, what clothes they're wearing, and every movement they make onstage and more often than not it comes across that way, whereas with Elvis, he just did it, effortlessly, unselfconsciously, without thinking about it. Above everything, the lyrics always travelled through his brain and then back out through his mouth. He always sang the lyrics of the song"

At the end of the first rehearsal it had been decided that Jerry was definitely part of the group. There was no discussion - he was simply the right person for the job.

Then there was the matter of a keyboard player. As James recalls: "Glen D was not available for the first time that we opened in Vegas, but I'd done an album with a producer and writer named Shorty Rogers, a sort of jazz player and a great arranger. I had a call to this jazz album he was doing, and I met this keyboard player, Larry Muhoberac, who was fantastic. Larry played a great solo on this song we did, and I was talking to him during a coffee break and I said man, it's a real pleasure to hear you play piano and he said, 'the pleasure is mine as well'. We kept on talking and I said I don't know if you'd be interested in anything like this, but Elvis phoned me and asked me to put a band together to go to Las Vegas. And he said 'sure, I'd love to do it' so we put it together.

"I had some drummers in mind as well. The drummer who played with Ricky Nelson, Ritchie Frost, was a super player who played on all of Nelson's hit records. He was just a great player, so he came in and played the show great. We played a couple of songs with Elvis and when we took a break he came over and said I love this music and I really enjoy playing it, but I don't want to work this hard. I really appreciate you keeping me in mind, but I'm pretty close to retiring from the stage"

"Larry and I were talking after this and he told me he knew a guy in Dallas, a great guy and a great drummer who wanted to move to LA. I said he should give him a call and see if he was interested, so he did, and it was Ronnie Tutt. Larry and Ronnie had worked together in the Memphis area and the Texas area, so they were quite good friends. He called Ronnie who came out to do a little audition. We also had a couple of other drummers to come in and audition"

One of those drummers was Gene Pello who, for a very brief period in the rehearsal studio looked almost certain to be Elvis' drummer. Pello wanted the gig really bad - and told that to James after he'd auditioned. But unlike the situation with Jerry, James and Elvis wanted to try out a variety of players.

Jerry recalls watching what happened that day at auditions: "Gene Pello was an LA session player originally from New York. He had played on some Motown hits and was a very strong drummer with lots of chops. Pello was the only one out of the bunch of drummers that came down there to audition that had the power and the energy so when he played, all of Elvis' guys – including Red West - were going, this is it, this is it. And Pello was picking up on all this and got the idea that he was getting the gig.

" It was an amazing scene. When we finished playing, all of Elvis' guys were over there shaking his hand. All the gophers were giving their approval. Elvis liked him okay because he had the power and the chops to do it. Then Larry Muhoberec stood up and said "wait, hold it, hold it, my friend Ronnie Tutt just flew all the way out here with his drums to audition and he's been sitting over there all night. I looked over and there in the corner was this guy I hadn't noticed earlier. Elvis was cool and said okay, go and set up Ronnie. Gene Pello is watching on. Ronnie set his drums up and we started playing. Two bars into the song and as if like magic happened everybody knew that Ronnie was it.

"I remember it was very poignant because you could see Gene Pello's face dropping. He knew. He had all the strength, but he didn't have the feel that Ronnie did. I felt so bad for him."

Ronnie, who was sitting quietly in the corner watching Pello play and the response he got from team Elvis, had the feeling that the decision about the drummer had already been made before he was asked to set up his kit.

"Everyone was looking around at the so-called stage at that time and obviously thinking well, we finally got a guy," he says.

"They'd been rehearsing for a couple of weeks by then and had gone through a lot of drummers. I guess they were getting a bit tired of it, so after Pello played they were thinking oh, I think we've got a drummer. so, So when the last note of the last song was hit, they started putting their instruments away in cases and everyone was getting ready to leave. Then Larry goes over to Colonel Parker and says, this friend that you just flew in . . .' and he hit him in the purse strings and reminded him that he'd paid for Ronnie's ticket.

"So, the Colonel went over to Elvis and calls the guys. I could see a bit of head-to-head going on. They were all reluctant to get playing again but then they looked at each other and accepted that they had to do it. The minute we first started playing he Elvis looked around at me and was transfixed by the situation we were creating. We held that connection until the last note we hit together. The rapport that we had was the reason Elvis was so taken by me. He said later on, 'you know, Ronnie, that other drummer was good' – but he really didn't know how to speak in sophisticated musical terms, he just spoke from the heart – 'you know that other drummer is good, but you watched everything I did. I could look up at any time and I could see your eyes and I knew you were with me.'"

As with Jerry, Ronnie wasn't too fussed about getting the chance to perform with Elvis. He was planning on moving to the West Coast and with his reputation there wasn't much chance that he wouldn't find work. He and Larry had been working in the jingle business in Memphis and Dallas, and now wanted to give it a shot in Los Angeles.

“That was the land of milk and honey at that time", says Ronnie.

“Larry however, who is a good friend, advised me that everyone in the entertainment business would be there to see this show because Elvis hadn’t performed in ten years, so it’d be a great way to break into the Los Angeles scene because everyone would see us, and he was right. Everyone came and of course immediately I had a friendship with Jerry and James and the other guys, and one recommendation led to another and things started happening”

Years later Ronnie admits that he had no idea what to expect when he walked in to audition for Elvis’ band. He’d flown in for the audition with his kit and that was it. But, in a very common reaction, he was floored the moment he set eyes on Elvis.

"Some people have it" he smiles. “I don’t know how you really describe charisma, but he definitely had it. He had that presence. He was striking physically, and he also had a smile and a sense of warmth, and you could see the little twinkle in his eye. It was that sense of humor and look that said, ‘I’m here and I’m laughing at the whole thing’.

Glen D Hardin joined the T.C.B. Band in 1970 for the second season in Las Vegas. In the August of 1969 band, Larry Muhoberec had played piano but then decided that he didn't want to do it anymore, preferring to stay in Los Angeles and work on other projects.

"The boys had tried to get me to play with Elvis the first time as we'd worked together before, but I was tied up with other projects and just couldn't do it," Glen recalls.

"When Larry decided he didn't want to do it again, I decided I would. I was arranging music at that time and that was about all I was doing. I didn't play the piano at all anymore and I really wanted to get back to it. I was sick of being behind schedule with the music arranging. I love arranging music but the easiest thing I ever stumbled into was playing piano, so I decided I wanted to get back to doing that and it worked out real good because I not only played for Elvis, but I started arranging music for him. I arranged a lot of the things that were on the show."

In the 1950s Glen had been fortunate enough to see the young Elvis perform three times when he visited Lubbock, Texas. Like everyone else, he hadn't escaped the constant barrage of Elvis on the radio over the years.

"I remember that people said that the first time he played there he was paid something like $75," Glen says.

"I believe the gig was on a flatbed truck at a car dealership. The second time he played there I think he was paid around $600 and then the third time, which was just a short time later, he got $3000 - so things were changing and happening for him really quickly."

Glen's first impression of Elvis when they met was an immediate sense that, "he was just great and very friendly. He was real trim and just looked great. I had to audition. They had a list of people they wanted to audition, and I was on the list, I knew the boys wanted me to do it, but I still had to impress Elvis.

"He was just so easy to get on with at the audition. We sat down and started playing. He started doing some of his old songs and couldn't remember some of the words. Maybe he was just thinking about something else. I was just sitting there playing and singing the words to him, so he obviously thought I was okay and knew my stuff.

"When we first started rehearsing with him, we spent a bit of time together. He booked long rehearsals. I think he liked to rehearse, and he also liked to hang out with the boys. We spent a lot of time at rehearsals just taking breaks and arm wrestling and sending out for cheeseburgers and all that sort of thing, but we'd also get a lot of work done. At one time or another we ran through every song he had ever done, at least touched on it briefly, so that if it ever came up, we would know it."

So, was Elvis any good at arm wrestling? "He was pretty good," smiles Glen. "He was a lot better than me."

According to James everything clicked the first time the T.C.B. Band rehearsed together.

"It was just great," he says. "We played and the feel and energy were there right from the start. The more energy you can put into it the better it is, and we had that, so it was a great feel. Then when you added Elvis, who had such a strong voice, it was amazing.

"We played tunes like Mystery Train, Heartbreak Hotel, My Baby Left Me and Shake Rattle and Roll, songs that had energy. Plus, we did a few ballads like Love Me Tender. It just felt good to Elvis and all the band members"

One subject all of the T.C.B. Band members are reluctant to discuss in detail is how much they were paid for their time working with Elvis. It has been suggested that some members were paid more than others were but none of the T.C.B. Band wants to discuss that, even now. They do, however, agree that none of the figures suggested in other books written about themselves and Elvis have been totally accurate.

"I doubt whether we were all paid the same," says Jerry.

"In (Peter) Guralnick's book he has some figures but they're not true as far as I'm concerned.

"After the band was formed, we were all independent agents. It wasn't like there was ever a leader of the group. James put the band together, but we all made our own deals over pay rates and everybody played whatever they wanted to play. There was nobody saying, 'you need to play this here and you should do this.' That just wasn't the way it worked."

CHAPTER 4

LADIES AND GENTLEMEN…
ELVIS PRESLEY

Chapter Four

Elvis opened in Las Vegas in Las Vegas on July 31, 1969. He had flown from recording sessions in Memphis to sign the as yet uncompleted contract for the engagement in February, doing it amidst the construction work for the stage at the International Hotel amidst a blaze of publicity.

The first act to appear at what was being touted as the world's largest showroom was Barbra Streisand who would open the room earlier in·July. It wasn't until April 15th that he actually signed the real contract as the Colonel continued his trademark publicity campaign that included posters, banners, and balloons, along with one hundred thousand 8 X 10 glossy photos, fifteen thousand color portraits of Elvis and many other promotional items.

As the date grew closer Parker's publicity campaign became even more intense, even though the season was 80 percent sold out by the beginning of July. The Colonel didn't like to take chances. The night Streisand finished her engagement, the Colonel and his team of gophers moved into the Showroom and overnight readied it for Elvis's first show.

Opening night was an invitation-only affair. The owner of the International, Kirk Kerkorian, flew in actor Cary Grant who joined the likes of Fats domino, Paul Anka, Pat Boone, Phil Ochs, Carol Channing, Shirley Bassey and Dick Cark in the audience. The Colonel flew in a plane-load of critics from New York and Elvis sent an invitation to Sam Phillips, his mentor from the Sun Records days.

This was obviously an enormously important night for Elvis - one of the most important performances of his career. If the show worked, it would be a triumphant rejuvenation for his career.

If he flopped? Well, no one really wanted to think about the consequences of that.

He was very nervous says Ronnie Tutt of the atmosphere backstage on opening night.

"The only time I ever saw him get really nervous and moody about performing and saw how it obviously affected all of us around him was opening night. A few things hadn't gone right in the rehearsals and that added to the tension."

Showtime was 8.15 as the curtain went up for the Sweet Inspirations who were followed by comedian Sammy Shore. Neither was particularly enthusiastically received. The audience was there for just one performer - Elvis Presley.

And then it was time. Elvis hit the stage, plunging into Carl Perkins' Blue Suede Shoes and the entire room at the International exploded. This was Elvis at his finest, augmented by a ferocious band who knew the true meaning of rock'n roll and how to deliver it.

The set that night continued with I Got A Woman, Love Me Tender, Jailhouse Rock, and Don't Be Cruel before Elvis spoke to the audience: "Good evening, ladies and gentlemen". Welcome to the big, freaky International Hotel, with those weirdo dolls on the walls and those little funky angels on the ceiling and, many, you ain't seen nothing until you've seen a funky angel. Before the evening's out I'm sure I will have made a complete and utter fool of myself - but I hope you get a kick out of watching."

The show continued at a relentless pace. Cary Grant was on his feet applauding, the comedienne Totie Fields was dancing on a table, wine bottle in her hand, and all of the hotel's waitresses were staring wide-eyed and lustily at Elvis.

As Ronnie remembers, the TCB's first time onstage with Elvis in Las Vegas was extremely exciting.

"Besides all the hoopla, or whatever you want to call it, that was made out of it the first show, there was also this excitement of what we were doing. My image of Elvis at that particular time was that physically he was in the best shape I ever saw him. He looked like a black panther out there, almost like an animal. He was so sleek, and the way he moved and that we moved with him and the music moved us in time together was just amazing."

Those sentiments are echoed by Jerry who still considers the opening night of the first Las Vegas season the highlight of his time performing with Elvis.

"You have to understand that one of the things with Elvis prior to that night is that he hadn't really done much performing in front of people for a long time," he says. "He'd just done patches here and there and he really didn't know how people were going to react, especially in Las Vegas as he'd had funny experience there before and hadn't done so well.

"We were with him in the dressing room before the show started and Elvis was extremely nervous. I think one of the most poignant moments I ever saw onstage was when we went out on that stage that night. We were just standing there, and the audience went wild. Through the first and second number of the show the transformation in Elvis was just astonishing. You could see the change in his facial expression and muscle tone. It was very physical thing. Essentially it was the transformation of someone going out there not knowing what to expect. By the third song it was amazing. It was simply Elvis realizing that this was where he wanted to be and that this was what he wanted to do. This was it for him."

Unlike a contemporary stage set up, for these shows in Las Vegas, the T.C.B. Band and Elvis never had monitors onstage, hence they learnt very quickly to perform by listening to and watching the interaction between each other. These were rudimentary shows.

Aside from the absence of monitors and other onstage technical enhancements, there was virtually no backstage augmentation either. In other words, no catering! As Glen laughs, "there wasn't even Coca Cola at the gigs."

Joe recalls that the backstage rider was a case of a diet soft drink and a case of regular soft drink, but as Jerry points out, it wasn't that important: "We were never there. We didn't need it really."

Thirty years All these decades later it's fascinating to hear the T.C.B. Band members reflecting on those early shows with Elvis, particularly in light of how the technical side of rock'n roll shows has changed over the years.

Jerry: "We had very little in the way of proper equipment in those days."

Ronnie: "We never even had a band stand on the stage. We set up right on the stage with the drums flat on the floor. Jerry was on one side of me, James on the other and Elvis in front. We might have had a small drum riser in Las Vegas, but certainly not when we were touring."

Jerry: "Am I just looking through rose-colored glasses or was it nice playing without monitors? We stood close together and we didn't rely on something artificial to know what we were doing and to hear each other."

Ronnie: "The only thing that was hard to hear at times was the keyboards. But we all listened to each other in close proximity. Elvis stood right in front of us because he was digging it too. He loved to stand right in front."

The lights focused on Elvis were particularly harsh and were the partial cause of eye problems he developed towards the end of his life.

"They were brutal," Jerry says. "A lot of the arenas had low sightlines. I know that because I stood behind him and there would be four or five spotlights blaring directly at him. That's why he had to have such glittery jumpsuits - there was no real lighting."

Then, of course, there were the costumes which continually changed, varying at times from pea soup green suites to those with Indian braiding down the sides. The process of selecting the stage clothing was, not surprisingly, fairly erratic.

James: "We would go to places and have someone bring out all these patterns. We didn't have a lot of time to pick and choose. It was pretty much a case of selecting a color and style we liked and getting the shop to make them up for us."

Ronnie: "In a way the stage costumes were embarrassing, but you've got to remember that it was Las Vegas. The whole idea of the look we were going for was a combination of something showy, something that would look good, something that would fit well, something that was practical - but at the same time it had a look that I think the music itself spoke for. It spoke of a little bit of gospel, a little bit of country and a little bit of rock in roll. We played a bit of everything and I think we tried to get our wardrobe to mirror that."

Joe: "My guys in the orchestra used to call the band The Polyesters. There was no way they were the T.C.B. Band. They were the Wash-n-Wears."

Jerry: "I was in charge of selecting the colors each night. Charlie (Hodge) would come down and tell me what Elvis was wearing that night and I'd get the word to the guys that we were wearing dark blue or whatever it was. We all had quite a few suites. We had two whites, two blacks, and turquoise. We had a lot of rhinestones. We must have had ten rhinestone outfits made. We even had a one-piece suit."

Glen: "That was the jumpsuit. I remember saying to one of the guys one night "excuse me while I go and slip into something less comfortable." The first wardrobe we got was a Segals. I was down there, and I found these shirts that had a fringe. We had them in black, and white, and wore them with a pair of black or white pants. Then we all went out and got Italian boots."

Joe: "I went out and brought the band vests the second day so we wouldn't sit back there in those Las Vegas tuxedos. We had purple busts instead."

James: "You know, the stage costumes didn't worry me. It did bother some of the other guys, what with the rhinestones and flares. For me it was interesting and pleasing that Elvis wanted us to look like a group, his group. It was Elvis and All The King's Men. The T.C.B. Band. And TLC - Tender Loving Care - for the ladies."

The Las Vegas shows worked to a formula. The Sweet Inspirations would come on with their own band and do a set of about 45 minutes. They'd be followed by a comedian, and then there'd be an intermission followed by Elvis and the T.C.B. Band. The shows weren't long, Elvis's performance ranging from a shortish 45 minutes to a more typical hour. However, if Elvis was enjoying himself a lucky audience might get a 75 minute show.

There was never an encore. Once Elvis left the stage that was it. He was in a car heading to his hotel or the airport within minutes of the show finishing.

"For security reasons he didn't want to hang around," Ronnie says. "He had told me stories of the early days and he'd learnt his lessons well. If he got out late to the limousine or was delayed for some reason the fans would literally tear his clothing off and patches of his hair away from his head. These were the '60s and '70s, not the '50s, but at the same time you never know with an audience exactly what a crowd is capable of under those particular circumstances. I know, for example, that he had to tape his rings on so that people wouldn't tear them off. He had fingernail marks and claw marks all over him if he'd been caught after a show."

As Jerry recalls: "The show was just one solid hour and goodbye. There were no encores, no nothing. He'd disappear immediately after he came offstage, which is where that thing about 'Elvis has left the building' came from. People would rush the stage the moment he finished. I remember one show we had a temporary stage and people got underneath it and started rocking it so hard that we had to get off quickly before it collapsed. Elvis had already left the building, but they thought he was backstage. It was frightening."

And, let's make no mistake, the T.C.B. Band with Elvis were loud - like loud - onstage. Certainly, it was nothing that Las Vegas club audiences had ever experienced before.

"It was always intense," says James. "There was the excitement of the show and the audience building up to an explosion. It was like that every night. Every night when we walked onstage, we really didn't know what was going to happen. There was always lots of energy coming from the audience. They were always brilliant and loved everything. They screamed so hard that often we couldn't even hear Elvis. Basically, we always knew where we were in the song, but it got to a point sometimes where the actual noise from the audience overpowered the stage sound."

As Jerry recalls those early shows: "Well, we didn't use monitors. It wasn't like stacks of Marshalls. James was using pretty much what he uses now. When we started with Elvis, I had this bass amp and that sat over by itself between Ronnie and the piano. Sometimes on solos I cranked it but during the main part of the show we had a pretty good balance. Back then I could hear just about everything going on onstage."

Adding to the musical picture was Joe who'd joined as orchestra leader and conductor when Elvis returned to the Las Vegas International Hotel.

"This was Elvis' second time in Las Vegas," Joe recalls. "On the first season I wasn't with the group, but I'm pretty sure they weren't happy with the conductor they had then. I'd taken over the band at the International Hotel and had brought in a lot of new players, including some really hot guys from New York.

"Originally, I was offered a job at the International, but I had other clients that I was working with at the time like Florence Henderson and Diahann Carroll. Later I got a call from Tom Diskin in the Entertainment Department. He called me at home and asked if I'd like to conduct for Elvis and I told him that would be part of my gig because I was now working for the hotel. I was not an Elvis fan by any stretch of the imagination.

"Tom Diskin said that I should come to Los Angeles and meet him and the Colonel and that's what I did. I was certainly capable of doing what they needed doing. Let's face it, for me doing Hound Dog was not exactly a musical experience! I came out of a whole different world and this was totally different musically.

"The first thing we worked on was the motion picture That's The Way It Is. Glen D. and I got along from the moment we said "hello". Anyway, Joe Esposito came over at the first rehearsal and said Elvis was coming in and that I should meet him. It was no big deal for me at all. But you know, from the time I said hello there was an electricity there. I could see exactly where he was coming from. We rehearsed a few things, and everything was precise and happening. The eye contact with Elvis gave me a feeling of confidence that it was all going to happen the way it should.

"There was something special about Elvis. I'd worked with a lot of so-called headliners and stars, but he was something very different. His charisma went to the back row at any place he was playing. At that point the International Hotel was the largest showroom in Las Vegas. It sat 1,200 people, but it wasn't so much the size of the audience, but the reaction. I've sat on that stage with a lot of people, but I've never seen a reaction like it outside of Gladys Knight and The Pips on a Saturday night for the Black Schoolteachers Convention. When Elvis was onstage the power would just vibrate through the back wall of that room."

In hindsight it's interesting to hear the T.C.B. Band's views on what made them and Elvis such a ferociously powerful combination. It's a factor they still struggle to fully explain.

"It was much more than just another gig for us because Elvis was such an icon and a huge idol around the world and in the music industry," James says. "It was really an honor for me and I'm sure everyone else felt the same way. He was such a wonderful entertainer and a great artist. The energy you felt when he was around was just incredible. He just had so much charisma.

"The chemistry in the band worked right from the start. Ronnie's such a great player and all the band are superb musicians. It had a lot to do with the fact that we all worked so well together. Our background in music was very similar to Elvis' background, so it was like a marriage in that respect as well.

"The thing about Elvis' show was the intensity and the energy and everything that he projected along with the band and the singers. Everything was just so perfectly tight."

Part of that tightness was because of Joe's role, one that was particularly hard as he was coordinating numerous musicians onstage. One very famous story concerns his feelings about working with Elvis, particularly in the early days in Las Vegas. It's known simply as The Marbles Story.

"After the first show in Vegas, one of Elvis' guys asked me how I enjoyed working with Elvis and I told him it was like following a marble falling down concrete steps," laughs Joe.

"That obviously got back to Elvis because the next day when I came to work and opened the door of my dressing room - there were marbles all over the floor. The sink was full of marbles; there were marbles in all my clothes pockets. Written on the mirror was, 'follow the marbles - EP.'"

Much later there'd be another prank played on Joe, probably at Elvis' instigation. It was in Buffalo, which was Joe's hometown.

"Every time we played my hometown, Elvis would give me an extra sentence during his introduction mentioning that it was the town that I came from. One time we arrived at the auditorium, and the dressing room was like a men's room. There was a small corner with the urinal in it and they'd filled the urinals with ice and roses and left a note saying, 'welcome home Joe'."

The audiences, both in Las Vegas, and at the concerts around the States were, not surprisingly, completely crazy from the moment Elvis came onstage until the moment he departed an hour later. The stage quickly became littered with all manner of objects hurled by the audience.

"There were lots of knickers and hotel room keys and notes," Jerry recalls. "I remember a couple of un-used Tampax. I believe they were un-used. None of us examined them that closely. Then there was stuff like teddy bears. I have a photo of Elvis standing right in front of my amplifier and we're both laughing because there's this little teddy bear peeking out from behind my amplifier. It had been thrown onstage and someone had walked back and stuck it on my amplifier."

In James' recollections there were very few stressful times during the shows. An exception was a slight disappointment sometimes when Elvis pulled a song from the set that all the band members enjoyed playing.

"Still, even when that happened, we had to remember that it was Elvis' show and the King of Rock in Roll must do as he feels," he says. "He pretty much had the show under control, and we were so tight as a group that we could adapt to any changes very quickly, so it didn't really matter what song he wanted to do.

"The thing for us was just the excitement, the energy and the reaction of the audiences. We had tourists coming from Japan, sometimes two 747's a week, maybe four. The Japanese fans were just unbelievable. There was one little girl who came over to Elvis at the front of the stage. She hugged him and whispered in his ear and he started laughing. The band were looking at each other and wondering what was going to happen next, and then she jumped onstage and ran over and grabbed me and kissed me and hugged me. Elvis got the biggest kick out of that. He thought it was so great and we talked about it for a week. Little things like that which you didn't expect happened all the time and that was part of what kept it so interesting for us.

"There was no way of knowing what Elvis' reaction would be to someone from the audience. Occasionally he'd get mad at someone in the audience who'd start calling out for songs he hadn't got to, but not very often. He liked to surprise people with the songs he did."

There were few times when female fans made it onto the stage, the majority of times they just rushed to the front of the stage and waited - and hoped - that Elvis would come over in their direction.

"That was mainly a security thing," continues James. "They tried to keep it from happening as much as possible. There were some incidents that happened over the years. Some guys jumped up onstage one time and the security people had to tackle them. It got to the point after so many different things happened onstage that everybody started to get a little gun shy."

There was a constant stream of people who wanted to get to Elvis' suite after a show or were telephoning him or the T.C.B. Band and leaving weird messages. Some of them were a lot more than weird, beginning with the first time Elvis received a death threat during a season in Las Vegas.

"It got real scary," James admits. "In fact, after the death threat the hotel told Elvis that they would understand if he didn't want to go out and perform the show that night. They had F.B.I. men and Memphis Mafia and police all planted in the audience.

"The main worry was when Elvis sang You've Lost That Lovin' Feeling. What he would do in that song was turn his back to the audience and there'd be a little pin spot on the back of his head. The room would be dark except for that little spotlight on his head and everyone figured if someone was going to try and shoot him it'd be during that song.

"So that night we started doing the song, but it had been decided that they wouldn't take the lights all the way down. Elvis had refused the suggestion to not do the show. He said, 'I can't worry about that stuff, I can't let this bother me and I must do the show.' He was certainly wary but was adamant that he had to perform."

Jerry: "They had trained people, FBI people, watching at the show. It was quite heavy. From what I recall someone sent a threatening letter that was written on a real cheesy black and white Xerox photo of Elvis and it had a knife, childishly drawn sticking out of his face. The experts looked at it and decided that it could be serious. At the show that night . . . I think it might have been Sammy Shore the comedian. After he'd done his bit onstage he went and sat with friends in the audience and when Elvis came out Sammy stood up and put his hand out to shake Elvis' but it looked, particularly in the semi-darkness, as though someone was pointing a gun at Elvis and at least twenty guns clicked on him from security in the room.

"That wasn't the only tense moment or time over the years when Elvis received threats. One time there was a doctor backstage waiting with oxygen. Everything was set up just in case something happened. They had everything covered.

"There were often some weird times with guys in the audience too. There were guys that got off on watching the reaction between Elvis and the women in the audience and I suspect they would have liked to have watched Elvis in bed given half the chance. And on the other hand, there were guys sitting there who just had poison in their eyes because they were so jealous of the way women, often those that were with them, responded to Elvis."

Soon after the T.C.B. Band had started their first Las Vegas season, James introduced a little trump card for his onstage appearance in the form of a pink paisley guitar.

"That guitar was an incredible thing," James says. "When Fender called me and told me they had this new guitar for me I asked them to send it. They said there was no way they'd do that - I had to come down and get it. I saw this guitar and, wow, it was flashy. I couldn't see myself playing it because I'd never played what you'd call a real flashy guitar like that. I took the guitar to Las Vegas, but it took me two weeks before I got the nerve to bring it out and play it onstage. Until that point, I was playing an original 1952 Telecaster guitar that my Mum and Dad bought me.

"In Vegas, Red West had kept telling me I should play the new guitar, so finally one night I decided I would go for it. Elvis was singing Johnny B Goode and was joking around with one-liners, so he wasn't paying any attention to the guitar. Then it was time for the solo on that song and he looked around and did a double take when he saw the guitar. I almost stopped playing waiting for his reaction. I didn't know what he was going to say. In fact, he didn't say anything during the show, but afterwards he called me to his dressing room and asked where I'd gotten the guitar from, so I told him that Fender had sent it to me. I went on to tell him how I was afraid to pull it out, that I didn't want him to embarrass me onstage by saying something about it being a terrible color, but he loved it, so I stayed with it and he was happy."

Particularly during the long Las Vegas seasons, things, understandably, became a little predictable for both Elvis and the

T.C.B. Band. To relieve the tedium of endless shows and performances in the one venue, the band and Elvis developed a variety of fun onstage antics to keep themselves amused. One of Elvis' favorites became known as Stump the Band whereby he'd attempt to fool the T.C.B. Band by starting a song they didn't expect and see if they could lock into the music. Given the background of the T.C.B. Band, it should have been obvious to Elvis early on that at least one of them was going to know a little of any song he threw at them - but it didn't stop him trying.

"He tried and tried and tried," laughs Glen. "But I don't think he ever stumped us. I remember one time when we were playing the Forum in Los Angeles in July. Elvis was about as far away from me as he could get, on the far end of the stage, and there was a curtain partly obscuring him. He leaned down to kiss a girl and she must have whispered in his ear and asked him to sing Blue Christmas. This is in the middle of summer mind you. So, he raised back up and started singing 'I'll have a Blue Christmas . . .' and we went straight into it. The funny thing was that, and this is important, you had to watch him every minute because if you took your eyes off him something would happen. You'd miss something because he was all over the place onstage, up and down and walking all around for the entire show.

"He moved a lot; all the time and his body language were very important. The funny thing though was that if you watched him, he was easy to read. He really knew what was happening and he might stop a song just like that, but if you were watching him, you'd know what all of his motions meant."

Elvis realized right from the beginning of his association with the T.C.B. Band that they were indeed a special group of musicians and perfectly suited to the way he wanted to re-invent his career as a live musician - and he went to great lengths to make sure they realized how important they were to him - and to keep their loyalty. Often that reinforcement involved significant gifts for the musicians. Glen recalls one night when Elvis walked into tour rehearsals carrying a huge pile of boxes containing digital watches.

"Those watches cost $500 a piece in those days because they'd just come out. I knew that's how much they cost because the price tag was still in the box! Elvis started giving one to everybody at the rehearsal. That night there were a few invited guests who he also gave watches to but before he got around to giving a watch to everybody he ran out. So, he told the people who didn't get one to come back the next night and he'd have a watch for each of them. And that's exactly what happened. He arrived at rehearsal the following night with another stack of boxes and came and asked everybody if they got one the night before, and if they hadn't, he gave them one of these $500 watches."

There was another instance where Elvis was handing out watches to those around him when Jerry was the one T.C.B. Band member who didn't receive one.

"Elvis had been giving out watches to people and there were these ones with the words 'Elvis Presley' printed on the bezel like what corporations do when they put their names on things for publicity purposes. Elvis thought this was cool and was handing them out. A few days later one of the guys told Elvis that his wasn't working that well and Elvis turned to him and said, 'I don't fix 'em son, I just give them away.'

"Anyway, I didn't get one of these watches and I asked Red West why. He said that Elvis had mentioned to him that I never seemed to wear the jewelry he gave me, so I didn't get a watch - and that's one thing I would really liked to have had."

Throughout their time with him, Elvis continued to be extremely generous to the T.C.B. Band members. All of them had their T.C.B. (Taking Care of Business) pendants, which had been a gift from Elvis. At one stage, Joe's broke and he gave it to Joe Esposito to take back to Memphis to get repaired.

"The next week they brought it out to wherever we were it had been repaired and there was a small diamond in the middle of it," Joe says. "He also gave me a crucifix once which I gave to my mother. You could stop vampires with that thing."

As a rule, all of the T.C.B. Band members were given the same gifts. Jerry feels that he reserved the big presents, particularly cars, for either people he was apologizing to or for people from his intimate circle.

"There was one exception," adds Ronnie. "I was called up to Elvis's suite, into his bedroom, one night after a stint of concerts in Vegas. I'd been ill with some weird infection that the doctors couldn't diagnose. It made me as weak as a kitten. During that time, we were doing a lot of strenuous shows, but I stayed out in Vegas for them. Elvis knew I was hurting and struggling to do the shows. When I arrived at his bedroom, he was nervous because that's just the way he was with things like that. He was a man of few words. He just said, 'well, I know how difficult it has been for you Ronnie, but you stood in there and I appreciate you keeping the energy up and I want you to have my favorite star sapphire ring.' He loved black sapphires and it was a ring that was his and he wanted to give it to me. It meant a lot to me on a one-to-one basis. It had nothing to do with the value of the ring, it was his heartfelt personal appreciation. I'll never forget him taking it out of his hand and giving it to me. I was so moved because it was something he really liked to wear."

One constant throughout all the touring and recording the T.C.B. Band did with Elvis was his respect for the musicians in the band. He looked after them and most of the people close to him. According to all the T.C.B. Band members, there was never any suggestion that Elvis reassessed what he was doing and considered getting other musicians to play with him. He was too loyal to the T.C.B. Band to even consider such a move.

Ronnie: "Loyalty was a really important thing with Elvis. He liked to have people around that he was comfortable with and who he felt were the very best. He would introduce us from the stage and say things like 'here's the best and most expensive group of musicians in the world.' He took pride in being able to say that, even onstage."

Joe: "He had a different respect for these dudes than he did for the other people that worked with him. There's no contest - the other people, like the Memphis Mafia, were his dartboards. These guys in the band were his career."

Jerry: "If you left him to go to work for someone else, he wouldn't hire you back, but if you left him for other reasons it was cool. I needed a break at one stage and left for two years and that was cool with Elvis and he was happy to have me back. But if I'd gone to work for someone else that would have been it. He took things like that as a personal slight."

Whilst Elvis always treated the T.C.B. Band incredibly well and let them know how much he respected them, the same could not always be said for his attitude to the Memphis Mafia.

As Ronnie recalls: "He'd lash out at them within a second. That was just the way he released his nervousness. But when he respected you and your musicianship, he didn't take anything out directly on us. We never saw that, but we were certainly aware of his nervousness."

Jerry is another T.C.B. Band member who doesn't recall the Memphis Mafia with too much affection.

"I'm not a male bonding kind of person," he says. "I'm not the kinda guy who wants to belong to a club. I'm not into that now and never have been. But those guys were something different. That was their whole trip, the male bonding thing. Red, Sonny and some of the other guys had been together since high school, so they certainly bonded with Elvis. In many ways he needed them but, on several occasions, he indicated to me and other people that he knew exactly what was going on. In other words, what he was saying was that he could tell these guys that black was white and they would defend that idea to the death. In reality he knew exactly what they were all about.

"They never treated me badly, so I basically stayed away from them. I didn't want to be mixed up with them and I didn't like that whole scene at all."

According to Glen "they were nice guys, but you wouldn't want to be their enemy. Red (West) got some guy in an elevator one time and the guy couldn't get away from him and he beat the guy up real bad. The guy had been driving a bus and trying to get into Elvis's place and somehow or other he got on a ledge and tried to come through a window. Anyway, Red worked him over pretty good."

At times, members of Elvis's entourage would try and become involved with aspects of the live show, which didn't impress either Elvis or the T.C.B. Band.

"It was usually Sonny West or Lamar Fike," James says. "Lamar was the worst. He would always be saying, 'Elvis wants you to do this song, man. Why don't you take this song out and put this one in?' So, we'd try it in rehearsal and naturally it wouldn't work for Elvis' set. Lamar would always be out in the audience at rehearsals yelling for us to do this and do that. It was usually because he wanted to get rehearsals over quickly so he could go to some restaurant and eat all the food.

"I remember one time in Las Vegas, Lamar was out in the audience whilst we're putting a show together which is being filmed. He's hollering things at us and Elvis was getting pretty uptight with him. We were rehearsing In The Ghetto and Lamar yells "kick it off James, kick it off". I don't know what made me do it, but I kicked off the song and Elvis said, 'hold it James, no-one is going to tell you when to play'. Elvis picked up his mic stand and told Lamar to get out of the rehearsal."

Joe: "Technically Elvis never had a lighting director. Lamar used to do it and to be honest it looked like a jailbreak at Alcatraz some nights. I brought Bob Kiernan in and he was the first person to give Elvis a proper lighting plan."

Incidents involving confrontations with people around him were, however, rarities but Glen certainly recalls the occasional times when Elvis appeared nervous and uptight before going onstage because he felt he hadn't done enough preparation.

"I think he would sometimes feel like he hadn't prepared enough or something like that. He did like to rehearse, but often if he wanted to try some new things that he hadn't done before, he'd get nervous. But then he'd walk onstage, and all that nervousness would disappear, and he would become real loose and easy. He'd always have a good time."

Surely, however, there must have been times when the band saw Elvis in a particularly bad mood for one reason or another?

"Just occasionally we'd see that," Ronnie says. "Elvis had a great sense of humor. There were times I must say when he didn't have the greatest sense of humor about things, but that was rare.

"At one stage Elvis got in the habit of throwing a little bit of water at us. He always had glasses of water handed to him and he had gotten into the habit just out of being silly. You must remember that we were doing two shows a night, and three on the weekend. And every time we went to Las Vegas we were there for four to six weeks, so after a while we were just like caged animals. And from time to time things got a little crazy, so onstage Elvis started taking a little water and flicking it over us. It was just a casual 'hey, are you awake' thing. He started doing it to me and Charlie Hodge first, and then moved on to Glen D. After a while we decided that we'd had enough and that we'd get our own back on Elvis, so we went out and bought water guns. We all had them with us onstage, so the minute he flicked water on one of us we all stood up and started letting him have it with the water guns. Normally that would have been the kind of thing he would have loved, but on stage that night, he didn't quite see the humor of it."

Then, as James recalls, Elvis decided to get his own back on the band by getting his own water pistol.

"One of the road crew came up to me before a show and told me he was thinking of passing this water pistol to Elvis on stage and did I think it was a bad idea. Sure enough, during the show that's exactly what he did, and Elvis started shooting at some of the band. He came up to me, but he didn't shoot water at me because I was holding an electric guitar. I talked him out of it, but he went on and shot water at John Wilkinson and Glen D. Elvis really liked to play little games onstage. He really enjoyed that.

"There was always so much noise with the audience screaming and hollering and everything else going on, so Elvis would mutter jokes and asides to us. One night he burped into the microphone and quickly said "that was the best meat I had all day." He was always making little inside jokes to us."

Ronnie also remembers a night when a collection of little wind-up hound dogs were released from the side of the stage and allowed to wander across in front of Elvis and the musicians.

Again, to keep things interesting, Jerry casts his mind back to times onstage when Elvis asked each member of the T.C.B. Band to play a solo after he introduced them.

“I had to follow Ronnie Tutt," he laughs. "How the hell does a bass player follow a drummer? I figured that instead of trying to out-flash Ronnie, which I wouldn’t be able to do, I’d just play a slow blues thing. Elvis would come out every night and say ‘Jerry Scheff, play the bass, play the blues Jerry’. So, I’d play the blues. Then, when we were in Louisiana one time, I realized I was sick of playing the blues, so I told everyone in the dressing room, but not Elvis, that when he introduced me, I wasn’t going to play the blues, that I was going to play a Cajun riff. So, Elvis comes out and asked me to play the blues, but I went into this other thing and he looked at me kinda strangely.

“The next night he said, ‘Jerry Scheff on bass . . . what’re you going to play tonight Jerry?’ and I went off and played the Cajun thing again. A couple of nights later he came out and said again, ‘what are you going to play tonight Jerry?’ and I said, ‘I think I’m going to play some Wagner’ and I went off into that, so it got to be like a little running joke.

"Then I set it up with David Briggs, who was playing with us at the time, and I told him that when Elvis asked me what I was going to play, I was going to say that I was going to play the piano. I’m sure if that had happened, he would have said, ‘okay, let’s see that’ because he knew I couldn’t play the piano. I had set it up with David, who was going to be under the electric piano. I would go over and it would seem like I was playing even though I wasn’t. Briggs went and snitched on me so what finally happened was that Elvis came out and went ‘Mr. Jerry Scheff - what are you going to play Jerry?’ and I said ‘I'm going to play the piano Elvis’ and he said 'play the blues Jerry' so we had a little running thing about that."

As far as Jerry is aware, the audience was more often than not acutely aware of the onstage joking that was going on between Elvis and the members of the band.

"There were always two shows going on," he laughs. "There was the show for the audience, but there was always this insider thing going on onstage."

During the shows, one of the constant sources of inter-band amusement was rhythm guitarist Charlie Hodge who had known Elvis longer than anyone, but from all reports wasn't in the same league as the other musicians.

"Charlie just stood there," Jerry smiles. "He really didn't do anything. He had a good time, but even when he was singing, they didn't have his microphone turned on. It wasn't plugged in, but he pretended that he was singing. Once in a while, I think the sound guys did put up a harmony of his with Elvis. As a guitar player, just forget it, he'd stand there and when we were playing loud, I didn't hear what he did but, on the ballads, he'd get full of himself because he could actually hear what he was playing and all of a sudden, he'd start playing louder. I'd be listening, and time after time there was Charlie chugging away on his guitar. I asked him many times not to play, but he just kept on going, so one night I brought some wire clippers onstage. One of his jobs was to give Elvis his glass of water or a scarf and when he did that, he'd throw his guitar on the ground. So, one night I went over and cut his chord, so he was playing the guitar, but of course there was no sound."

Joe: "Wasn't that beautiful. It was the best the group ever sounded! Charlie really played those cowboy changes on the guitar, and Glen's charts didn't have cowboy changes. Charlie came out of a 1-4-5 world of guitar playing and we were well beyond that shit. He had stalled at Music 101."

Jerry: "I can remember one time when I was taking a really ridiculous drug that caused flatulence. Onstage I let one go. It was a terrible smell and Elvis walked back to get his towel from Charlie and, as he said afterwards, it felt like he'd walked into this green cloud. I just pointed at Charlie and said, "it can't be me; it must be Charlie." Stuff like that happened all the time."

Elvis was constantly prone to whims during the Las Vegas shows. One incident that still amuses the T.C.B. Band was when he decided that he wanted a gigantic gong onstage. Somehow, he became aware of the location of the gong that had been used in some of the J Arthur Rank films.

"It was over on the MGM lot in Los Angeles, so Elvis decided he wanted it right dead center on the stage," laughs Glen. "He thought of it in the middle of the night. I think it was after the show one night when we were all partying. Anyway, a lot of people had to get on the phones and start getting people out of bed and getting a truck to move it to the hotel. They got it and they bought it over to Las Vegas the very next day.

"The song we were going to use it in was I Just Can't Help Believing. We had this little guy, a percussion player. He was a little pipsqueak of a guy who weighed about 100 pounds. Elvis told him 'when I get to the end of that song, and I move my hands like this, I want you to hit that thing as hard as you possibly can'. The guy said he would. We were doing the show and it came to that song. The guy drew back and hit that gong as hard as he could. But instead of the desired effect, all that happened was that the blow spun the guy around and threw him out into the string section, knocking over people, violins and music stands.

"The thing is that you have to warm up a big gong like that. You need to get it going with some mallets and then you hit it. Obviously, the guy didn't know that because when he hit the gong it just spun him around. I think they broke some violins and it was a terrible mess. It was wonderfully funny though. It was certainly the funniest thing that ever happened onstage."

Joe Guercio continues the saga of the gong: "Every city has a place where you rent instruments. Bo Mahoney, a Dixieland drummer, had a place in Vegas called The Drum Shop and he rented anything you could possibly need. He heard that Elvis was coming to town and that there was going to be a gong used in the show. Bo buys one because he figures we'll end up renting it from him. He put it in his window a month before Elvis is due in town and doesn't get as much as a nibble on it. Elvis comes in and he brings the gong from MGM, so it's obvious that Bo is not going to rent his gong, and he's stuck with this thing in his window. Then they took the gong back to MGM because they needed it for a motion picture, so I called Bo and asked him if he had a gong for rent. I already knew he had a gong to rent. He says, "have I got a fucking gong for rent, you bet your ass I've got a gong for rent". I asked him how much it was to hire it for a four week engagement, and he said, "I don't give a fuck what you pay me, just get it out of my store."

If the gong wasn't enough Elvis later decided, on Glen's suggestion, to get a large harp onstage.

"I was up talking to Elvis one night," Glen laughs. "I said 'you know Elvis, what we really need here is a big old beautiful harp right up there, pretty much in the center of the stage. It'll look so beautiful.' Elvis liked this so he called Joe Guercio over and told him to have a harp organized for the next night's show. Joe spent hours on the phone because I think harp players were a little hard to find at the time, particularly in Las Vegas."

Throughout the early years of playing in Las Vegas none of the T.C.B. Band can recall any totally disastrous performances.

"There was never a bad performance in those days," Glen says. "Things sometimes became a little weak when the drug thing came along. By then he wasn't singing with all that strength and he was walking through the show. So, I can't say that there never was a bad performance, but I don't think there was ever one so bad that people got up and walked out. But they did walk out one night but that was something else entirely.

"There was one night in Las Vegas where Elvis got into a mood where he was laughing all the time and he was making up words as he would go along. They were funny words and he did that at the early show, and I think again in the late show. You have to remember that all of these songs were somebody's favorite song and, believe it or not, people were somewhat offended. They'd come to a show and Elvis is doing their particular favorite song and there he is messing it up and putting in a lot of funny words. He was just laughing all the way through these shows. I don't know why - I guess he was just in a silly mood, but one night 800 people got up and walked out and asked for their money back. The Colonel had a little talk with him about the economics of it all and, of course, he never did it again. Elvis really didn't want to upset his audience, but just this once he was in a silly mood."

Ronnie has another recollection of this night. "Elvis was open to suggestions of songs to play onstage. If we went to him and said, 'hey, we think it'd be a great idea to do this,' he'd listen to the idea and often he'd give it a shot. He'd try the song out and if it didn't work then it was oughta there. A few songs that were recommended were recommended for different reasons, particularly at recording sessions. The idea was to get them to the point where they'd be recorded and then we figured that if they got recorded, we might be able to get to play them onstage because it'd obviously be seen as helping promote the new record. Elvis would always try new songs and if they bombed, well, they were gone from the set list the next night.

"I remember one time in Vegas when we opened with a completely different show. Elvis had paced the whole show differently. He wanted to get away from C.C. Rider and That's Alright Mama which were the normal opening songs with that kind of beat and feel. I can't remember exactly what it was he opened with, but the whole show was like that. He wanted a complete departure from anything he was known to do. It was all new material or previously recorded material and I could see that he was really nervous about it. After a few songs I could also see that he was not getting the response from the audience that he had anticipated, so the next night it was back to the way it had been before. We never did a show like that again. Elvis would always go back to what was comfortable for him - but you've got to respect him for trying different things."

Sometimes, however, the band became concerned that elements of the show hadn't been rehearsed or prepared sufficiently.

"Elvis would have me write charts and sometimes we would do them unrehearsed which used to scare the shit out of me," Glen says. "I remember when I thought that the horn part in Trilogy hadn't been transposed properly and it was possible that the horn player would stand up in the middle of the show and blow it. I talked to Elvis about it later and said, 'man, you've got to stop this because sooner or later something's going to happen'. That very night I was walking down the hallway. I had this big stack of music like I so often did, and I thought while I had a few spare minutes, I might as well check something out. The first cello part I looked at was written in the wrong key. That set me off right there."

Regardless of those occasional glitches, the T.C.B. Band established a formidable reputation as possibly the tightest rock in roll band in the world at the time. Prior to playing with Elvis they were all known as stellar individual players, but together they were untouchable.

"It was later in the piece when I realized the international influence and impact, we were having as a band with Elvis," says Ronnie. "We obviously went out there every night in Vegas and gave it everything, but it's really hard in that environment to know what impact you're having. There'd be reviews in Rolling Stone, Playboy and local newspapers and magazines, but it really hit me when the results of a poll were published in an English magazine. In every category each of us were top in the category for the instrument we played. I was the top drummer out of all the drummers in bands that were touring at the time. James was the top guitar player. Glen D was the top piano player, and Jerry was the top bass player.

"Then they had a category for Best International Artist, and they had us down as number 3 behind Stevie Wonder and Paul

McCartney. That was weird because we didn't have records out. It was amazing to know that people were paying that kind of attention to what we were doing because we were just out there playing, and we weren't trying to push our individual careers or doing records. We were just there."

This recognition in Europe was, in Jerry's opinion, a little different to the way the T.C.B. Band and Elvis were perceived in their home country.

"In the States, the feedback I got from the music business was that the people who liked Elvis music liked the early Sun stuff and thought it was sacrilege for there to be anyone playing behind him except a three piece trio like it was in the 50's," he says.

"Not only that, but they thought what we were doing was way over the top - which it was if you look at it in the context of the 50s stuff. What we were doing was something completely different to everything going on around us. Nobody was doing anything like that at the time. We just came out blasting. No-one was doing anything like that at the time."

Ronnie: "It was the only concert type show of its kind at the time. It was something Elvis had envisioned in that dream before he started playing in Vegas and it came to fruition because of his perception and because he knew what he wanted. Since then, we've all seen so many acts who go out on tour with background singers, strings and a band set up like we were, but Elvis was the first guy to ever do that. The first, so it did have a major impact, and I've gotta say that people throughout the industry would hire us to back them up on records because they liked what they heard of us playing with Elvis."

Whilst touring with Elvis, the T.C.B. Band had very little to do with Colonel Parker, the majority of their business dealings being done with his assistant, Tom Diskin. Still, the band were close enough to observe the relationship between the Colonel and Elvis during this period, particularly the tensions that arose between them over the nature of the live performances at this time.

"It was a strange thing, a love/hate thing," Glen says of the interaction between Elvis and the Colonel. "Elvis used to say he was going to fire the Colonel, but he never did. I think he just had a feeling that if he did the whole thing, it would just come crashing down. I don't know why he would have thought that, but I heard him say it a number of times. But he did talk pretty ugly about the Colonel at times.

"Elvis didn't let the Colonel interfere with the music at all. He was tired of doing things the Colonel's way. He had done all that movie bullshit and he was sick and tired of all that, so he wasn't going to let the Colonel have anything to do with the show or the music or the band or anything like that. As a matter of fact, when the Colonel found out how much we were getting paid it really annoyed him. He told Elvis 'you know boy, I could put some monkeys behind you onstage and we'd sell just as many tickets.' We heard the Colonel tell Elvis that."

As Glen recalls: "We actually had no dealings with the Colonel. We all made our deals individually with Elvis. For example, I have no idea what the other guys were paid. I kind of have a pretty good idea, but I still don't know for sure. We all played a lot of sessions before we joined Elvis, so we had to replace that income. It was pretty easy to make a deal with Elvis.

"After I'd rehearsed with Elvis he said, 'come out here in the hall, I wanna talk to you' so we went out in the hallway and he said, 'man, I love how you play, let's make a deal. I want you to work for me.' I told him that was fine and what I would charge, and he said, 'that's fine, that's good.' That was it. We shook hands and it was done. Every time I asked for a raise, Tom Diskin would say, 'oh no, there's no chance that we can raise your pay' and I'd always reply by saying, 'well, tell Elvis I really enjoyed working with him.' Tom Diskin would then tell me that he'd call Elvis and talk to him about it. Then five minutes later, the phone would ring, and he'd say, 'it's all set, you've got your raise.' I can tell you; he didn't talk to Elvis about it."

Jerry explains that all of the band had to be particularly careful what they said around Elvis.

"The simple thing is that if you asked for something within earshot you were likely to get it," he laughs. "We all knew that basically at any time we could go to Elvis and tell him that we needed something, and we'd probably get it. But I don't think any of the guys took advantage of that."

More of a problem was having to discuss money with either the Colonel or Tom Diskin.

"There were times when they'd call up and say that we were going out on tour," Jerry says. "I'd remind them that I was due for a pay raise. Tom Diskin would tell me that they were paying top dollar now, and that expenses were up. I just told him to tell Elvis that I'd really enjoyed working with him. So, an hour would go by and the telephone would ring, and it'd be Tom Diskin telling me I could have the extra money. I doubt whether it ever got to Elvis because neither the Colonel or Diskin liked being confronted with having to discuss something like that with Elvis."

Occasionally, there'd also be scheduling problems which would cause conflict between the T.C.B. Band and the Colonel and Tom Diskin. James remembers all too clearly a time when shows he was doing as a member of Emmylou Harris' Hot Band appeared to conflict with some Elvis dates. How Elvis responded to the situation says a lot about how Elvis felt about the T.C.B. Band.

“There was a time in 1976 where I had a tour with Emmylou which was fine because we had extra time off from Elvis. I was in Europe with Emmy and it was planned that after those dates finished, we’d go back to the States and continue the tour for a few weeks before hooking up with Elvis again. The Colonel had gone ahead and booked a tour for Elvis during the time we were meant to be finishing the dates in America with Emmylou. He’d forgotten, or chose to forget, that we had this time off from Elvis.

“Tom Diskin called my home and spoke to my wife because I was in London. He asked her if I’d received the contract for the two weeks of shows and she told him that I definitely had not. He really wanted to speak with me, and my wife gave him a number in England, but as we were travelling so much, I didn’t get the message. When I returned to LA, he called again asking if I'd received the contract. I told him I hadn't, and he acted surprised and assured me he'd sent it. I had to explain to him that I was not available to play with Elvis during that time, but I told him I'd speak to Ed Tickner who was Emmylou's manager. I was suffering serious jetlag at the time and I thought Tom Diskin was very rude to me in the conversation. He told me that unless he had an answer from me, he'd have to get another guitar player.

"That night I went to bed and asked my wife not to wake me, but at 10.30 that's exactly what she did. She told me there was a phone call that I should take as it was Elvis on the line. I picked up the phone and Elvis said, 'James, I understand that you're not going to be able to make this two week tour that's coming up.' I explained to Elvis that I thought we had time off, so I'm taken the work with Emmylou. Elvis got very upset with the Colonel's office because I think he felt there had been negligence on their part. He said to me, 'I assure you that if you can't make this tour then we'll cancel. The tour will not happen without you.' Fortunately, it worked out fine and Emmylou was able to get Albert Lee to play guitar so I could leave to go back to Elvis. I think that Elvis's attitude says a lot about how he felt about the band and me personally. I was very honored.

"For me it was a situation where I was the leader of the band and having put the band together, I had to make a decision and I felt more obligated to Elvis."

Things changed within the T.C.B. Band ranks in 1973 when Jerry quit the band.

"It got to where I was having a little too much fun," he laughs. "It wasn't all with Elvis, but that certainly had a lot to do with it. I was living in Los Angeles, but I got to the point where I needed to get away, so I moved to a little island on the West Coast of Canada. I had actually moved there in 1971 and bought a house. So, by 1973, I'd been living there for two years and I just needed to get away from life on the road. Elvis was very loyal. An important factor was that I didn't quit him to go and work for somebody else. About three or four times during those two years that I was gone, they called up and would say that Elvis wanted to know if I was coming back. Then in 1975, I was getting a divorce and moving back to Los Angeles. They happened to call up around then and I said I'd come back."

For every member of the T.C.B. Band there's no question that Elvis series of shows at Madison Square Garden in New York in 1972 was the highlight of their time together as a band.

"That was one of the highlights of my life," recalls Joe. "We had The Sweet Inspirations and Jackie Kahane, but the audience didn't want to hear any comedy. They wanted Elvis Presley and that was it, so they were heckling Jackie. It finally came to the second half of the show and I started the Theme from 2001: A Space Odyssey and you could feel the audience. I don't think I'll ever get the experience again. There was this huge rumble, rumble, rumble and by the time we hit the note where Elvis came out so many flash bulbs were going off from cameras that there were moments when it seemed like the entire Madison Square Garden was lit up. It was like someone had turned up the house lights, but it was just the blare from flashbulbs. I've never seen anything like it. This is Madison Square Garden. We weren't taking about Mrs. Murphy's Lounge; we're talking about a big venue. It was just unbelievable. It was absolutely fantastic. There's nothing like working Madison Square Garden with Elvis. That was his first time playing there and, boy, those New York people went absolutely bonkers. When they love you, they love you. It was like the Yankees winning a World Series.

"Elvis was really prepared for these shows. New York is always going to separate the men from the boys. He just knocked them on their ass. And when Elvis wanted to knock people on their ass they were knocked down - really knocked."

For Jerry the later shows at Madison Square Garden after his return to the T.C.B. Band following a two-year absence were also extremely special.

"When I went back to work with Elvis, they sent me a tape," he says. "I listened to it and I recall there were only one or two songs I'd never played so I learnt them and turned up at Madison Square Garden fifteen minutes before Elvis and the band were due to go on.

"Onstage Elvis turned around and said to me, 'Hi, good to have you back,' and away we went. I was used to the intensity, so when we started, I just hopped on to it. And then he literally turned around and motioned to me to slow down a bit. After about five or six notes, he'd picked up on what I was doing. What had happened was that the tempo and feeling of the show had settled back to where it should have been. Some of the stuff we were playing was like punk lounge music. It was so intense."

For some of the Memphis Mafia, the experience of playing in New York was a long way from their previous experiences. Joe tells a funny story about driving down 34th street towards the venue for a rehearsal.

"We had a New York band and New York is my town. The band was sensational. But one of Elvis' guys is in the front seat of the car says, "boy, if anyone ever told me I'd be in New York City and driving past the **Entire** State Building. 'I thought, does that sound like hillbillies? 'what the fuck am I doing here?'"

With the exception of the Madison Square Garden concerts, all of the T.C.B. Band have a hard time pinpointing shows with Elvis that really stood out. Such was the level of everyone's professionalism that the level of the performance was always superlative - there was rarely a bad show. Some shows were better than others, naturally, but the quality of the performances was constantly high.

"There were so many really good shows," Glen recalls. "Of course, I'll never forget the Aloha from Hawaii show. That was just wonderful. We started shooting that show at 2.30 in the morning because it went out live to the Far East. That was kind of unusual. We had rehearsed it over there in that very building that we played in. It was just very special.

"Madison Square Garden was very special as well. I remember thinking at the shows 'man, I've never heard him sing better.' I was really disappointed when the album came out from those concerts because they had sped it up slightly, but I don't know why. I think the Colonel did that, but it sounded terrible to me."

For Ronnie it's impossible to single out any one show as outstanding but, in his opinion, the quality did vary from night to night and often that had something to do with the audience on the night.

"What stands out about the concerts were the incredible highs and the incredible lows," he says. "Elvis was a very spontaneous performer so you would have these incredible nights where it was just roaring. People were packed to the ceilings and were responding wonderfully, and they'd get the show of their life. That's what he would do. He was very devoted to his fans.

"But if people were sitting on their hands and the acoustics were bad, or it was cold in the building, or we were in a real conservative town, it wouldn't always be that great. A lot of things contribute to how people respond and sometimes the response wasn't quite what we expected, and he'd turn to me and under his breath say, 'let's get the hell out of here'. That's just the way he was. The rest of the time we were kicking and urging each other on."

For James, the one show that stands out was the concert recorded and broadcast around the world from Hawaii early in January 1973 which became known as Aloha from Hawaii.

"That was the most special show for me," he says. "I love going to Hawaii anyway, but the overall feel of the show was amazing, what with the actual setting and knowing that it was going by satellite all over the world.

"The night before we did a very late rehearsal which went on into the morning. During the rehearsal I was sitting onstage. Everybody had taken a break, and Elvis was out in a room talking to some people like Marty Pasetta, the producer. I was just sitting onstage and playing around with melodies and tunes, particularly the Hank Williams song I'm So Lonesome I Could Cry. I was playing the blues and Elvis walked back in and up to the stage. He looked at me and asked what I was playing. I told him it was an old Hank Williams song and he started singing it. Then he called everybody up and said that he wanted to run through the song. He wanted to put it in the show, and he did.

"The same thing happened once when I was in Nashville recording with him in 1971. Chip Young and I would just sit around and play tunes. We were going through In the Early Morning Rain and Elvis came in and started humming and singing it and then he said, 'let's wax it, let's get it down on tape.' And that's what we did. He also recorded Suzie Q because he knew I'd played on the original version and he wanted to do it."

Understandably, some of the concert schedules, because they were so extensive, became a little tedious so both Elvis and the T.C.B. Band, had to work hard at keeping the shows interesting for themselves. One way Elvis did this was to vary the song list for shows - usually without telling the band.

"We always had a set list, but you could be sure there were going to be some surprises," laughs Glen. "We could be sure that what was on the set list was not the show we were going to do.

"Elvis would just sing whatever came into his head. If he thought of a song he hadn't sung for a while, but wanted to sing that night, then he'd do it. There were some songs that he'd sing just once a year. He'd go into a few older songs from time to time like Wooden Heart and Return To Sender and some of those other old things, but he didn't do them as a rule."

According to Glen, the fact that Elvis was always throwing little surprises into the set meant that it rarely became boring for the band members. Certainly the work load for Elvis, The T.C.B. Band, and the other singers and musicians was grueling, particularly during the long seasons in Las Vegas or Lake Tahoe. The usual schedule was two shows a night and three on weekends. The first one began around 8pm in the evening with the T.C.B. Band appearing an hour later and performing for an hour. Then there'd be a break, and the second show would start at midnight, with the T.C.B. Band coming onstage at 1am and performing till 2am. They'd be out of the showroom by 3am and ready to party till daybreak.

"We didn't get too bored because Elvis kept it so different most of the time," Glen says. "And also, the crowds would be different. With the early show people would just have had a big dinner and they'd be just a little bit quieter. The late night group of people would be drunk and ready for anything so everything would be loose and a lot of fun for the second show.

"It was meant to be the same performance for both the early and late shows, but it didn't work out like that. Elvis would always make it somewhat different. There'd be some songs we'd exchange or do differently. Some songs just fit better into the late show than they did the early one, and with the crowd being all crazy for the second show, it was certain to be different."

Even when Elvis pulled out some bizarre song choices, or ones that the T.C.B. Band and the other performers didn't like, they'd never complain. It was after all Elvis' show and what he wanted was what happened.

"A lot of them we didn't like," says Joe. "There would be double takes onstage when he called some of those tunes. But he'd do them because someone in the audience called out for them, or simply because that's what he felt like singing."

Jerry: "We tried to be as supportive as we could be and if he liked a song that much, we'd give it a shot. And the truth is that if it didn't work the song would usually fall by the wayside anyway. Elvis had a pretty good sense of what was getting a good reaction and what wasn't."

James: "When we rehearsed, we'd pretty much have a great line-up of songs and of course we had our set list onstage. Now, if we were lucky, Elvis might do the first three songs on the list and from then onwards you never knew where he was going. Guercio was always tearing his hair out because if Elvis did something different to what was on the set list all the orchestra had to get different charts out. Elvis didn't care about that. Guercio tried to explain it to him, but Elvis said, 'Joe, I want to do what I want to do when I want to do it,' and really it was Elvis's show, but if you think about an orchestra back there with charts, well, it became very tough for Joe. But certainly, every show was different, and you never knew what to expect."

Ronnie: "One night when we tried to do a completely brand new song for an opening night the audience didn't respond in the way Elvis was used to them responding so we dropped that one."

Joe: "Once we changed the introduction and it went straight in the toilet."

According to Joe, "Elvis was one of the best big venue acts I've ever worked with. A lot of those big acts have ramps that go out into the audience so they can be closer to the crowd, but Elvis just walked out there and grabbed them. You could feel the energy from the back row. I've worked arenas with major acts and the kind of vibe you pick up is that you're only entertaining half the house downstairs and maybe a few people upstairs, but with pretty much every show Elvis did it worked for the whole place."

Whilst it seemed that on every occasion Elvis left the audience completely satisfied, there were certainly some shows that earned the audience's collective gratitude more spectacularly than others. For Ronnie, it was the large arena performances that worked best.

"Elvis would always do a good show and was dedicated to that, but there were lots of times when it was much more than just good, and the audience were just blown away. When the audience was really responding, Elvis would really get into it, and that often happened at the arena shows where there'd just be incredible highs. The Vegas shows had both highs and lows."

Joe: "Opening nights were highs in Vegas, but after that it just became a job."

Ronnie: "Opening nights were definitely the highs. They're obviously great, but I would say that consistently the arena shows were the more exciting ones for Elvis."

Jerry: "I have a theory about that, and it's that the show was too intense for a smaller room like what we were playing in Vegas. People would sit there, and they would look like they were numb. At the end of the show they'd go crazy, but during the actual show it was almost as though you could see their hair being blown back from the intensity coming offstage."

Ronnie: "I think that's true. I think the other thing that contributed to it was the fact that in most of the early days we did two shows a night. That ended up being changed in the last couple of years, but when we'd be doing the two shows we'd be out there onstage rocking out and there's people sitting there having their steak dinner right in the front row! The ticket was for dinner and show and that was ridiculous. That wasn't the way Elvis liked to perform."

As Ronnie recalls, if Elvis was likely to get upset during a show it was at the dinner performance.

"He would look around and be really annoyed if a waiter dropped a plate full of silverware or something like that. He would make some comment to the audience or us. He tried to make light of it and would never get really nasty about it - but on the other hand it was really insulting to him."

Throughout the T.C.B. Band's time with Elvis, he frequently talked about wanting to tour outside of the United States. He told the band this was the main reason he bought one of the airplanes he owned. He wanted to have his own plane for travelling overseas so he wouldn't have to be worried about security problems with fans at airports.

"He wanted to tour outside the States really bad, but the Colonel just wouldn't do it," says Glen. "I know promoters in Australia used to offer him a million dollars for a performance, but Elvis didn't really want to do those gigs where they put him out in the middle of a football field. He'd rather play at venues where people could be close enough to see him. But it didn't matter because the Colonel didn't want to do it. He used to say 'why should we go all the way over there to make a million dollars when we can just stay here and make a million dollars. I know for sure Elvis really wanted to go overseas. He wanted to go everywhere.

"As a matter of fact, last year when we were all in Europe doing Elvis - The Concert, it occurred to all of us that it was really sad that Elvis never toured in other countries. He wanted to, and of course the fans everywhere wanted him to. It was also sad to think that we all did it and Elvis didn't. It's not only what's happened recently, but back then me and all the boys were working with other people and playing all over the world, but Elvis didn't get to do that. It must have been frustrating for him and I'm sure he must have got sick and tired of being in the U.S.A.

"We played down South a lot. We played Mobile, Alabama, Atlanta and places like that all the time. We were forever down there. They could, and probably would have just booked him till the end of time in the South. We all got sick and tired of doing it. It's a lot more fun to play in places like Australia, Japan and England but Elvis never had the chance to find that out."

Possibly the hardest aspect of working with Elvis was watching his physical deterioration towards the end of his life.

"It was very hard," says Ronnie. "Very difficult. I think what was interesting about it was we had seen him over the years to be one of the most resilient men I've ever known. We'd start rehearsing for something before we had a tour or a Vegas season to do and he might look out of shape and generally not be looking too good. But by the time opening night arrived it was if, as I've always joked, he jumped into a phone booth and put on the Elvis suit. Then all you saw was this wonderful, beautiful, powerful artist and entertainer and singer. Despite that perceived resilience, he was very vulnerable at times and had to cancel shows because of his voice.

"It was very strenuous having to do so many shows in harsh environments for singers such as Vegas or Lake Tahoe, but at the same time we never thought it was really serious.

"It was uncomfortable to watch it happen, but somewhere deep down we all thought it was going to be all right. I think that's why it was such a shock when he did finally pass on. I just can't believe that it finally happened in that sense."

A constant for the T.C.B. Band was the presence of the Colonel, Tom Diskin, the Memphis Mafia and the other people associated with the smooth running of Elvis' shows.

At the peak of Elvis' touring there were around 80 people in the touring party, travelling on three planes - the show plane, Elvis' plane, and the concession plane which carried the Colonel and Tom Diskin.

"I was on the concession plane one night," says Joe. "I must have been leaving early for a show. We were going to Buffalo and I wanted to get there a day early and spend an extra night with my parents. Diskin and the Colonel had garbage bags of rolled up dollar notes from the concession stands and they started emptying the bags on the airplane. It was only a five-seater but there was money up to my knees. They were both just emptying the bags and counting the money."

The money came from an array of Elvis souvenirs sold at the shows. In those days T-shirts weren't a big item, the merchandise being predominantly scarves, buttons, pictures and posters. The Colonel insisted that every poster by rolled so the people who worked for him were always frantically searching for rubber bands.

One particular occasion, the concession stands ran out of hound dogs to sell so there was a frantic search of the town we were in for more for the fluffy toys. Unfortunately, there were only teddy bears available so, as Joe recalls, the Colonel was frantically wanting to know if Elvis was going to do (Let Me Be Your) Teddy Bear that night so he would have a good chance of selling them all.

The main person looking after merchandising was Al Gavorn. The sellers would scream 'get your latest posters, ladies and gentlemen' following a fairground approach to their selling.

"These were hucksters," laughs Joe." They were wonderful. We'd be going to Baltimore and Al would say before the show 'this scarf tonight is going to be Baltimore Blue'. Then we'd be in Dallas, Texas and he'd be doing 'ladies and gentlemen, I just want you to know that these scarves, the color tonight is Texas Tan.' I used to kid him by saying 'don't forget Gonorrhea Green.'"

When it comes to the Colonel, all of the T.C.B. Band have terrific stories of his erratic behavior.

Joe recalls a show at the Pontiac Stadium, in Pontiac, Michigan in 1975 where one of the supports acts for Elvis was a bluegrass band called The Bodie River Mountain Boys.

"It was freezing and for some reason, because it was New Year's Eve, the Colonel made them wear diapers to be like babies. These poor guys were out there onstage freezing their asses off."

This was also the show where Elvis split his pants onstage in front of 62,500 people. The Sweet Inspirations immediately took over the center of the stage whilst an embarrassed Elvis changed, before returning to a standing ovation.

Always considering he was paying them too much; the Colonel was far from generous with the T.C.B. Band. In the early days the most he'd given them in the way of gifts was a metal contraption. None of the band can recall exactly what it was but suspect that the Colonel had been landed with a box of them and decided to appear generous by giving one of whatever it was to each of the band members.

Things began to look up when the Colonel came on the band's plane when they landed in Eugene, Oregon on Thanksgiving Day 1976.

"The Colonel made a big deal about how he was going to buy everyone Thanksgiving Dinner," laughs Jerry. "He had a stack of $5 bills and he walked around and handed everybody one note. He'd say, 'here boy' and give us $5."

Joe remembers that he never had any problems with the Colonel and was friendly with him till he died.

"The Colonel lived in Las Vegas. I never had a problem with him. In fact, his wife is still a very good friend of mine and we see each other at different functions.

"The way to handle the Colonel was to stay away from him. I guess everyone around him didn't particularly dig him, but it was just a business thing. I never had a problem with him.

"If the Colonel had never taken him out of Memphis, I don't think it all would have happened. The Sun Records people were good people, but it happened for Elvis when he was with RCA."

CHAPTER 5

"I DON'T KNOW WHAT YOU'RE DOING AFTER THE SHOW, BUT WOULD YOU LIKE TO COME UP AND MEET ELVIS?"

Chapter Five

Particularly in the Las Vegas years, the T.C.B. Band spent a lot of time hanging out with Elvis each night. There wasn't a lot else to do – other than hang out, go to the casinos or sleep. More often than not, after the second show, the band members would gravitate to Elvis' suite.

According to Ronnie, if you were in the T.C.B. Band or it was known that you were welcome, then Elvis' suite was the place to be.

"There were two areas there," he remembers. "One of the areas was his dressing room and then there was the party cum bar area and that's where I met a lot of celebrities that would come to meet him.

"There were all types, from singers to movie stars. A lot of film stars."

"Lucille Ball wanted to take me home,' he laughs. "At least that's what she told me. She said, 'you know I'm partial to drummers.' It just went on and on with all types of people."

It seems an endless parade of celebrities came to visit Elvis after shows, particularly in Las Vegas.

James remembers the night that Jerry Lee Lewis turned up for a show. "He sat through the whole show and never even acknowledged that Elvis was doing a show. He just talked to his friends right through Elvis' set."

Glen D had been in Elvis' dressing room before the show when Jerry Lee had barged in shortly before the show and Elvis was about to go onstage.

"Jerry Lee marched in and he reached over to Elvis and said 'Hoss, you gone all Hollywood'. Then, to make matters worse, he said to Elvis 'you know what your problem is - you let that crazy Colonel tell you what to do. I don't let no son-of-a-bitch tell me what to do.' Elvis turned red. He looked at Red and Sonny and said, 'get him out of here.' During the show Elvis stayed on the stage as far away for Jerry Lee as he could for most of the night."

Then there was the night that Sammy Davis appeared in the suite after a show.

James: "Sammy had a ring on every finger. Elvis looked at them and said 'Sammy, what you need is another ring' and then he gave him one."

Joe: "Elvis loved Sammy and Sammy loved Elvis. The first time I met Elvis was in Sammy's dressing room in LA."

And not everyone gets a call from John Wayne backstage after a show in Las Vegas.

"There was this night in Vegas when the phone rang in the dressing room," James recalls. "I think Joe Esposito took the call. Elvis got on the phone right there in the room with us and it was John Wayne. Apparently, John Wayne had a new movie that he was about to do, and he wanted to see if Elvis could play a part in this movie. Elvis called the Colonel down later to talk about it and the Colonel said, 'absolutely not'. He wouldn't allow Elvis to do it because he never wanted Elvis to play second billing to anyone."

A similar proposal, again in Las Vegas, came from Barbra Streisand.

"Barbra came down with Jon Peters," Joe says. "She had worked in Vegas the February before, but she came back to talk with Elvis about a motion picture. It was A Star Is Born, but I guess Elvis didn't want to do it because Kris Kristofferson ended up doing it and was marvelous."

In Las Vegas, Elvis had his upstairs suite where he stayed and slept. The Elvis entourage had the entire top floor of the hotel, with one wing being specifically Elvis' domain. This was the after-show hangout and the place where pretty much everyone involved with the tour would sooner or later end up after the night's shows.

"There was one night when Elvis wanted to tell us some stories," says James. "He could recite quotes from the Bible word for word. You'd go home and get your Bible out and there they'd be. He was a very religious man. and would sit down and tell us stories taking quotes out of the Bible.

"One night we were talking, and he wanted to tell us stories about being in the Army and when he went in as Private Elvis and they cut his hair off. He was one of the guys then. It was not like he went into the service as someone special. He went through the real thing. He would tell us stories about getting a weekend leave after working all week. He and his friends would party for a whole weekend and he'd just be wiped out. He'd come back and have to be on all night duty and was falling asleep. The other guys would come in and catch him sleeping. He really was just a normal, down-to-earth person. I don't think he really realized how huge he was in his music career. I think it was a situation where at any moment you thought he could go back to the farm and ride his horses and do his thing."

Whilst none of the T.C.B. Band were strangers to late night partying and drinking, Elvis was far more conservative. Whilst his latter-day excesses have been exhaustively documented, in the early days in Las Vegas and on the road, Elvis was, according to the T.C.B. Band, the epitome of control. Everything was laid out for the band, the Memphis Mafia and everyone's guests, but this was more as a courtesy on Elvis' behalf.

"There was always a bar in Elvis' room even though he didn't drink," remembers Glen. "He had a drink with me just one night. I used to come in to his suite and I'd go behind the bar immediately to make myself a drink and since it was his bar I'd say 'Elvis, can I make you a drink' and he'd say 'you know I don't drink' and I'd say 'okay Elvis'.

"One night I came in and as usual I asked Elvis if I could make him a drink. This time he said, "I want a glass of wine.' I thought he was kidding, so I made my drink and went over and sat down. He looked at me and said 'well, hey, where's my drink' and I said 'oh, I'll get it for you' and I got a glass of wine for him and he had a drink with me, so I felt honored about that. Mind you it took him about an hour to swallow down that drink."

As Joe recalls, “Elvis would have the occasional cigar and I think he’d drink vodka every once in a while.”

Jerry: “Believe it or not, Elvis was a straight lace kind of guy. He really didn’t look upon his medicinal needs the same way as someone skulking down an alleyway selling heroin.”

None of the T.C.B. Band make any secret of the fact that they partied extremely hard every night. As soon as the show was finished, they headed for Elvis' suite, or to the hotel bar or party in another room at the hotel where they were staying.

"We always partied," laughs Glen. "We always had a party. I only remember one time when I didn't get involved. I was so partied out that I just couldn't stand it. We were in Indianapolis and I actually went upstairs and went to bed after the show. But that was the only time I can remember doing that."

Amidst the endless late nights of drinking, laughing, singing and talking there's still one occasion that sticks in Glen's mind. It happened in Little Rock, Arkansas.

"They had us staying in a terrible old motel out on the edge of town. As we drove in there, we noticed that there was a liquor store right across the street. They sold mostly cheap wines and had signs painted on the windows advertising things like Banana Wine and Strawberry Wine for 59 cents a gallon. It was just terrible stuff. Somebody suggested we hit the store, so we did, and everybody grabbed a big jug of this cheap wine in each hand. We decided to have a big party and invite everyone we saw in the town. We'd also bought some expensive Scotch and figured we'd feed the girls all this cheap wine and then we'd have the Scotch for ourselves.

"Elvis had the corner suite in this place but he never did come over to the hotel. He just flew in, did the concert and flew right out. We knew he had the suite there so that's where we had our party. Sure enough, everybody in town showed up. There were just more girls than you could imagine, and everybody was getting bombed on this cheap wine and we just kept pouring it. It was a lot of fun. Anyway, it got real late - maybe 4 or 5 o'clock in the morning and the place was just a wreck so we decided that maybe we should clean the place up a little bit. Somebody got a big trash can and we put it over in the corner and we started picking up these bottles and throwing them at the trash can. As you'd imagine most of them didn't go in the trash can but hit it and broke. We were as drunk as you could be and we kinda didn't mean to, but we trashed the place. There was broken glass and wine and rubbish all over the place. Finally, we just left it there because I think we had to catch an early flight. So, we thought 'oh, this is going to be terrible, Elvis is going to get a big bill for us trashing that room.' But nothing ever happened, and it was never mentioned. I guess those people who ran the hotel just felt that Elvis always had a big party and wrecked the place, so they didn't say anything about it. Certainly, we never heard another thing about it again."

Equally memorable was a night all the T.C.B. Band still talk about when they had a huge party after a season of shows at Lake Tahoe.

"It was just a great place and we had a beautiful house to stay in," recalls Glen. "All the casinos up there own big houses on the lake and it's just wonderful. Anyway, Joe Esposito and Joe Guercio cooked up a real deal Italian meal this night. I can't remember whether Elvis came over or not. Joe Esposito called some sausage maker in San Francisco and told him that Elvis loved his sausage, so the guy sent about a ton of it over and it was good. The problem was that we were so high up that it took about two days to get the water boiling . . . in fact the altitude was such that we never got it really boiling. We invited everybody in town, and they all came. Joe had the limousine driver running up and down the hill to get things. They threw away all the plastic cookware and made the guy go and get wooden spoons and things like that. If someone needed a packet of cigarettes, they'd send the limo down the hill. It seemed like the whole night went on forever, particularly as it took the guys so long to get the water even close enough to cook that sausage."

Looking back on those days Glen laughs when it is suggested to him that it's somewhat amazing the T.C.B. Band members lived to be able to tell their stories some decades later.

"I don't know how we survived that time," he chuckles. "We made sure we had a party every night. Everyone would bring a bottle. Sometimes we'd lean on RCA Records for some party funds and usually they'd cough up some money, so we'd go to the liquor store and stock up on whisky. There were so many of us that sometimes the hotel would give us a party room and we'd just party away there."

The only member of the T.C.B. Band who didn't party as hard as the others was James. Well, that's his story and he's sticking to it.

"I never did party too much," he says. "I was just loving my music and playing my music. I was into guitars and cars and motorcycles. I guess that was pretty typical for the time. I just loved playing my instrument. At the time I never thought about what I was going to do next. All I knew was that if I was playing my guitar with someone, I was happy. That was my thing, and even after I'd get home at night I'd come up with little melodies and ideas, little things to keep the interest there.

"Everyone had to watch themselves on the tours, particularly with the one-nighters because all that travel would tire you out quickly. In this gig you have to be a little smarter than the other guy because you have to allow lots of time for rest and you have to eat correctly and pace yourself. You can party for three or four nights in a row, but then you really need a break. I had to learn that at a very early age.

"Sure, we partied and sometimes a bit too much. I pretty much knew where to cut off. I didn't want to hang with the guys too much because I knew how much work we had to do so I had to pace myself and rest, even when I didn't feel like it and would have preferred to have been out partying."

Whilst Elvis rarely partied with the T.C.B. Band when they were on tour, mainly because he'd usually left on his plane, the Lisa Marie, for the next city straight after the show, but when they were all in Las Vegas for an extended period he'd hang out with the band most nights.

"He was very social," says Glen. "He told us that if we wanted to bring friends up to his suite we certainly could. We were always welcome to bring friends. You'd certainly be careful not to bring some nut that might drive him crazy. If someone got a little too talkative, we'd get them out of the suite.

"Elvis always enjoyed meeting our friends and he'd talk to them. If he got bored with it all or was tired, he'd just go to bed. In Las Vegas he had a big old bedroom that was hidden away, and he'd just disappear and let the party roar on. It didn't bother him, and he wanted everybody to stay as long as they wanted to. It was great fun in Las Vegas because the sun would come up over the mountains there and it was just beautiful, with them turning purple and red. We watched the sun come up many, many times in Las Vegas. Many, many times."

Jerry: "The first year or two we'd hang out with Elvis a lot. We'd go down to the dressing room before the show and hang with him. He enjoyed that because he was always very nervous. Even if he didn't have a show to do his leg would always be moving. He was pretty hyper.

"One time he invited Glen D. and his wife and me and my wife up to his house in Los Angeles. Priscilla made chili that night. It was around the time when Elvis was really into guns. Whatever he was into he was seriously into it. Somebody told me that when he was into horses and being a cowboy, he had dust imported from Texas to throw on his horses and saddles. That's how much he would get into things. He was just inclined that way.

"So, at the time we had dinner at his house he was into his cop thing, collecting badges and stuff, and then he got into weapons. We were sitting talking at the house and all of a sudden, he'd say, 'look at this' and pull out a new gun from inside his sleeve. Then he'd pull another one from inside his trouser leg. He was really loaded down with hardware. Honestly, Elvis must have had six or seven guns secreted on his body. He just loved the stuff.

"At one point Elvis had to go to the bathroom which was next to the room where we were sitting. Elvis excused himself and we heard the bathroom door open. All of a sudden, we hear 'clunk',

'clunk', 'clunk' and Priscilla started laughing and said, 'it sounds like a knight taking of his armor doesn't it.' Evidently, when he went to the bathroom, he'd need to take off a couple of guns so he could pee."

Jerry explains that as the years went by the members of the T.C.B. Band spent less and less time with Elvis, but that seemed to be because of some things happening around him.

"It got to be almost a Howard Hughes type of situation where the people around him started manipulating access to him," he says. "One of the last times we played in Las Vegas, Charlie Hodge came down to where I was talking with Ronnie and said, 'Elvis is really bummed out that you guys don't come and hang with him before the show anymore'. Ronnie and I told Charlie that we'd been down a lot of times and every time we went down someone like Red West would turn us away and tell us that Elvis was busy. I'd even turned up at Elvis's suite after a show a couple of times and been turned away. Charlie obviously went and told Elvis this and apparently Elvis went ballistic and got really angry with the guys around him so from then onwards we had access to him whenever we wanted."

Naturally many of the more extreme fans would do just about anything to be invited along to a party in Elvis's hotel suite. There's one instance that still sticks in Ronnie's mind after all these passing years.

"I'd gotten to the elevator to go up to the suite and just as the elevator door started to close a girl jumped against the door and pushed it open with her hands," he says. "She had a wild, frenzied expression on her face, and she says 'I know who you are, and I know where you're going. You're going to take me there or I'm going to kill myself.' I said to her 'you might as well start doing it now because I'm not taking you up there, simple as that.'"

Whilst Elvis and the T.C.B. Band for the most part enjoyed the attention of the fans, there were definitely times when the more obsessive of them became an imposition on the band's freedom to move around and relax.

"The fans would keep coming up and knocking on my hotel room door, or having me paged," James says. "I'm sure they didn't mean any harm by it, but they were so persistent, and it became very annoying to not be able to go out of the hotel. I decided after the month when there'd been the death threat on Elvis that I'd like to stay out of the hotel, so I began renting houses. Glen and I stayed together in a couple of houses we rented. His family and mine both lived in LA, so we figured why not rent a house big enough to bring our families over. So, we did. We met this great lady who rented for everybody. A few years later, I actually ended up buying a house in Las Vegas."

James' frustrations with the more extreme fans are echoed by Glen who had his fair share of encounters with obsessive Elvis fans.

"They were a real problem because they'd try to get to us to get to Elvis," he says. "And it wasn't just women who wanted to meet him, there were people who had a song for him or a movie script or some sort of goldmine deal.

"The fans would drive us crazy. In the casinos back then they used to page people so when we'd come of a show and be sitting in the bar, you'd hear your name paged over and over again. On and on they'd go trying to get to you. You couldn't get up and answer the phone because it was almost always some nut trying to get to Elvis. It's a lot different now with Elvis gone. We can be friends with the fans, but back then most of them were just crazy and they'd do anything. You'd see them hanging around and they'd have all his albums they'd want signed and posters and pictures. When you saw them, you'd go the other way because if they tied you up in conversation you could be there for a long time."

Not surprisingly, Ronnie had very similar experience with extreme and persistent fans. Whilst he accepted that the majority were well meaning, "once in a while you'd get one or two that were overly persistent and sometimes you would have to get security to come on the floor and get them to stay away. There were lots of telephone calls and you really had to screen all your calls. You couldn't just pick up the phone when it rang, you had to get the operator to find out who it was."

Then, of course, there was always the problem of getting to and from the airport, a situation where Elvis and the band were most vulnerable to displays of rampant fandom.

"They always seemed to find out when we were arriving or leaving," James laughs. "It became a circus a lot of times because there were so many people involved in the tour that had to be transported backwards and forwards from airports. At times, we used decoys. Sometimes there were three different limousines to try and confuse people as to which one Elvis was in. They'd take Elvis out of the back of the kitchen of the hotel or a garbage can and then put him in the limousine. That happened a lot and it was often necessary just to get him out of the hotel.

"There was one incredible time I remember in San Francisco when fans just about turned our Greyhound bus over. We did a show with the Imperials and the bus was parked outside the venue waiting for gear to be loaded. There was a lot of it to be put on, so we were sitting and waiting on the bus for quite a while. One of the Imperials was sitting on the bus and the way he was sitting he looked like Elvis. People started screaming 'Elvis is on the bus' and the growing crowd of fans started rocking the bus. It got scary man. We were stuck in the parking lot and trapped. We finally got out, but it was real frightening."

Ronnie recalls a similar incident happening in Jacksonville, Florida. It is possible that James and he are recalling the same incident because one mustn't forget that this band toured extremely hard and played an enormous number of shows in many different cities.

"There were times when things would get a little tense in hotel lobbies and outside gigs," Ronnie says. "I remember coming out of a show in Jacksonville, Florida and we put a pair of Elvis-looking glasses on one of the Imperials, Joe Moscheo, who's a big, strong guy. We sat him low down in the seat and the people outside would go crazy as we were pulling out. There were hundreds of fans and somebody yelled 'Elvis' because they thought they saw Elvis in the bus. So, they were almost going to tip the coach over to get at us."

Surprisingly, given the amount of time he spent in the air, during the seemingly endless grind of one-nighters criss-crossing America, Elvis, was terrified of flying. He'd pull down the window shades on the Lisa Marie and try and pretend he wasn't in a plane, doing anything possible to camouflage the fact that he was 30,000 feet above the ground.

"Elvis didn't like to fly at all," says Ronnie. "That's why for all those years when he was doing movies out on the West Coast, he would always take a motor home. He'd drive all night long by himself. When we were in a car with him, he'd never let anyone else take the wheel. It was simply 'no, get away, I'm driving'. He loved to drive, and he hated to fly."

Whilst Elvis had moved on to the next city, the T.C.B. Band would stay in the city they'd just played for the night and travel early the next morning on the show plane which also transported the crew, lighting and instruments.

It was unquestionably a grueling schedule. Baggage call could be as early as 5am the next morning - and given the band's tendencies toward late-night partying, that would be frequently only a few hours after they'd gone to bed, if in fact they'd even slept at all.

Upon arriving at the next city, the crew would immediately go to work setting up for the next performance whilst the T.C.B. Band had the option of going back to bed or looking around at the sights and shopping.

"In the last few years Elvis saw how tiring that was for a few of us," says Ronnie. "To make things a little easier with the travelling, he asked Kathy Westmorland and myself to join him right after the show and fly with him. Immediately after the show had finished, we'd rush right out and go straight to the airport and ride with him on the Lisa Marie. He did that for Kathy and me for a while just to keep us in a schedule that was a little more bearable."

Ronnie actually met his wife Donna whilst on tour as she was one of the flight attendants on the T.C.B. Band's plane.

"She worked for the airline that we used to charter from," recalls Joe. "That was our four engine turbo prop plane. We'd get the same crew all the time and it became like one big extended family. We partied in that airplane. Everyone used to travel in the same plane, so luggage call in the morning used to be something like 6am. We couldn't leave the night before because the crew had to load all the equipment out of the venue and be on the plane as well, so we'd leave in the morning and when we got to the next town we'd lay down and die."

Elvis was also extremely approachable when any of the T.C.B. Band brought their families to shows. Ronnie remembers two occasions in particular involving Elvis and his children.

"My older kids came to his dressing room after a show. I had my girls there, and my youngest son, Ron Jr, and I believe my Mom was there as well. Elvis was being very courteous to my family and whilst he was talking to my daughters I looked over and saw Ron Jr. looking at him with this kind of strained expression on his face. Elvis, who was a very perceptive guy, saw this was going on too. Finally, when there was a break in the conversation, he leaned over to Ron Jr. and asked him if everything was okay. Ron Jr. looked up and said, 'how come you stand in front of my Dad all night long.' Elvis broke up when he heard that. He really thought it was the funniest thing.

"Elvis loved kids. When Donna and I had our first child, Elisia, we were having a natural home birth. I was the coach and so as we were playing in Las Vegas we had a pilot and plane on stand-by to fly me straight back to Los Angeles. So, sure enough, on December 7, I got the call saying that Donna was in labor. I zoomed to the airport and of course didn't play the show that night. I can't remember who stood in for me. The next day, after the baby was born, Donna and I got on the plane with our child and went back to Vegas. A few days later, we decided to take her into the dressing room as Elvis wanted to see her. He wanted to make sure I'd missed a show for all the right reasons! It wasn't really that he didn't trust us, more that he loved kids. We bought Elisia into Elvis' suite and he picked her up in his arms and held her for over an hour. He had the Lisa Marie waiting to take him to Colorado. It was warming up and Joe Esposito was freaking out and telling Elvis they had to leave. Elvis turned to Esposito and said, 'leave me alone'. He wasn't going to let go of our baby. That was a really endearing, touching moment."

The band was pretty stable but there were changes over time. When Jerry departed the band, Emery Gordy took over, and when he subsequently left, the bass position was taken by Duke Bardwell.

Glen was there for pretty much the entire period, finally quitting about a year and a half before Elvis died. David Briggs, Tony Brown and Bobby Ogdin replaced him in turn.

"It took three guys to replace me," Glen laughs years later.

Joe: "And none of them were as much fun. The thing is that this band had a marriage."

Ronnie: "When Elvis felt comfortable with something that's the way he wanted it to be. There was one other drummer that took my place, a great drummer called Larry London. I can't speak for myself, but what Jerry has told me is that Elvis wasn't comfortable with that change because it wasn't what he was used to with us."

As far as James remembers, he never missed a live show, but once had to cancel the end of a recording session because he and Glen had a show with Emmylou Harris booked in London.

"We were recording at Graceland," he says. "Elvis knew that Glen and I had to leave to go to London and he said it was no problem, but you couldn't really judge how much time Elvis was going to need you. Often things would fall behind schedule and it happened this time when Elvis wanted to record for one more day than what had been scheduled.

"Glen and I had to leave, so Felton Jarvis had to go and tell Elvis that we had an engagement booked in London and had to leave. Elvis wasn't happy with it, but he accepted that we had to go."

Glen recalls that he had told Tom Diskin before the sessions when he had to leave and Diskin had assured him that there was no chance the sessions would run over schedule. "I knew right then what that meant, and sure enough that very thing happened," Glen laughs.

Given the extensive and grueling tour schedules, the late nights and early mornings and general pressures of life on the road and in the studio with Elvis, it's somewhat surprising that the T.C.B. Band remained relatively close friends.

"I don't ever remember a full-blown argument," recalls Jerry. "I'm sure there were, but if there was it was kept under wraps. One thing is that it wasn't the kind of band where when we weren't working, we'd hang out together. I don't know whether you'd call it close friends in that sense. Close friends to me are people that have a bond where they share everything, even things that maybe their spouses don't know. But we certainly liked each other. I think that everybody on that show liked each other."

One thing aside from music that Jerry and Ronnie shared was a love for antiques.

"We were both into collecting antiques," Ronnie says. "We'd get into town early in the morning and Jerry and I would set out to see what we could find. We'd take our antiques that we'd bought and want to put them on the plane, but the Colonel would have our plane full of the antiques he'd bought which would piss us off."

It wasn't only in the early days that Elvis would regal the T.C.B. Band with gifts like the watches. Throughout their time with Elvis the T.C.B. Band were constantly given presents by Elvis, more often than not jewelry.

"That was just the kind of guy he was," recalls Glen. "He gave us a lot of jewelry and what was really nice about that was that when he gave us jewelry, he would always pick it out himself. He wouldn't go to a store and say, 'give me five of those rings or five of those watches'. He'd pick them out himself and I always loved the things he picked out for me, and I must say that I loved what he picked out for the other guys too."

For Elvis, these gifts were his way of saying thanks to the T.C.B. Band for the hard work they put in night after night and also keeping them loyal, something that was particularly important as he wanted to have a consistent touring band and all of the T.C.B. Band members were in constant demand to tour and record with other artists.

"We always got a bonus after every tour as well," Glen adds. "And it was always a good one, a real good cash bonus. Elvis used to come aboard our plane and he'd have the envelopes. He'd always personally hand you the envelope and shake your hand and say, 'thank you man, you played great as you always do'. That's just the way he was.

"As a matter of fact, if anybody ever made a mistake or was a bit sloppy after the show, if you'd mention it, he wouldn't even talk about it. It was past history. He'd say, 'oh man, to hell with it, we got their money' and then he'd burst out laughing."

Fans were a constant problem for Elvis when he was on tour as they besieged the airport when he was flying in, staked out the hotels, and mobbed him arriving and leaving shows. For the T.C.B. Band, things were a little easier because unless they were in the immediate presence of Elvis, they weren't so recognizable and therefore had a relative degree of freedom away from the stage.

"Most of the time people didn't know where we were staying," says Jerry. "The organizers of shows kept our whereabouts as quiet as possible. We hardly ever stayed in conspicuous places. A lot of times Elvis was in a different hotel, and unless he was in Vegas or New York, he didn't stay in really flashy places.

"Outside of the big cities we'd all stay in some big, sprawling motel that had a great pool and things like that. They'd put us in places where they knew we could sprawl out and hang by the pool and have some watermelon and fried chicken and cool out instead of staying in some flashy place. I liked that a lot. That was really cool."

A major event for the T.C.B. Band and the rest of the Elvis entourage were the end-of-tour parties which the band financed themselves.

"We had a fine system set up," laughs Jerry. "If we were late for the call to leave the hotel, we were fined a dollar a minute and that money went into a fund we would use to throw our own party at the end of the tour. It was hilarious. Sammy Shore would always write up a monologue and we'd all get together and do something crazy. There'd be a bar set and lots of food. We even had a costume party one night."

Elvis came to some of these end-of-tour parties, but a number of the band didn't really like it when he decided to accept the invitation.

"It was a bit of a dampener when he showed up," says Jerry. "He couldn't stand being there without entertaining, so the next thing you'd know he was on the piano singing gospel with the Imperials and we had to turn off the music we'd organized for the party. We were inundated with gospel music for the rest of the night.

"We still had a ball. One time Felton Jarvis got hold of a tiger jumpsuit. I think it was one of Elvis' old jumpsuits. He invited Elvis and Elvis came down and Felton did an impersonation of Elvis. Felton was brilliant. He could impersonate anybody. He had Elvis down perfectly with the stutter. He talked just like him and did this whole monologue as Elvis. It was a scream. We did things like that and it was a lot of fun."

On odd occasions, to keep themselves amused, Ronnie, James, Glen and Jerry would do gigs together, or, in various combinations, perform with other artists. John Wilkinson was the one member of the T.C.B. Band that would never get involved in these sideline diversions.

“There was a time when Elvis wasn’t working that James and Jerry and I would go out on weekends and do concerts with Johnny Rivers,” Ronnie says. “We got to be good friends with Johnny and, of course, his music was great, and he always appreciated musicians. We did those kinds of projects, including recording for other people. We did an album and a small tour with Tony Sheridan. In fact, there were plans to re-open the Star Club in Hamburg with him and us backing him. The album sold okay in Europe, but I don't think it was even released in the States. We did lots of things like that."

Beside his fixation for guns, during the 70's Elvis developed a number of off-stage fixations. The principal one was the sport of karate which heavily influenced many of his stage costumes and movements during these years and endured longer than anything else.

"Elvis was a man's man," says James. "He got into so many different things. He loved to ride motorcycles. He loved cars. He had his toys, his guns. Whatever he was into he went all out.

"Some of those interests came and went but the karate thing actually lasted to the end. He enjoyed it that much and it gave him a lot of discipline and control."

With the exception of Ronnie, the members of the T.C.B. Band didn't share Elvis' fascination with karate, much as he tried to get them interested. Instead he practiced and trained with karate experts who travelled with the entourage or members of the Memphis Mafia.

"I stayed away from it for a lot of years because I saw a lot of guys using it as an excuse to be one up on somebody," Ronnie says. "On the other hand, over a period of time we met so many people around us, whether it be on tour or in Vegas, who would be into it that I started studying it. So many karate masters would come through that I really found out a lot about the sport and the inner discipline and the mentality of it. It's known as self-defense but on another level that's what it was for me on stage as well because by learning about it, I was able to anticipate much more of what Elvis was doing on stage. I was able to relate to his combinations of moves and catch much more of what he was doing than if I hadn't been familiar with it."

And just how good at karate was Elvis? "Elvis was very good," says Ronnie. "Very, very good. He had this basic balance of hands and fluidity. What was interesting about Elvis was that once you get to the black belt level you get two or three more stripes and that's for what you bring to the art. Elvis brought a lot because he would get onstage in karate gear and people would take his picture and they would be shown all over the world. With such a publicized figure as Elvis he did a lot for the art.

"My son studies karate and I went to his Togo a few months ago. Master Chapman came out. He's about a six-degree black belt from Franklin, Tennessee. He showed me a copy of the number one karate magazine in the world and said to me, 'I've been studying karate all my life, and dedicated my life to it, and never made the cover of Black Belt Magazine.' I looked at the cover of the magazine and it was a picture of Elvis on stage with me right behind him, a big picture of my face. There I was on the cover. I think he was a little envious."

The other T.C.B. Band members were less than enthusiastic about Elvis' karate fixation.

"In Vegas he wanted everyone to take karate lessons," says Joe. "I think they all got given a white belt. Ronnie and Red West and Joe Esposito would have karate every afternoon. Vegas was my town and there was no way I was going to spend time taking karate. It just wasn't me. I couldn't have been an orange belt even if I tried. So, I didn't do it and I felt a very strange vibe for the first few days.

"At the end of that engagement in Vegas everyone was getting a belt. I think it was a white belt. Colonel Parker was giving out these things and he called my name. It's the closing night party. It still hangs in my office to this day."

Glen was another TCB member who didn't warm to Elvis' fixation with karate - and particularly his desire for the band members to learn the sport.

"That didn't interest me at all," he laughs. "When that got into the stage show it got real boring for me."

Elvis' karate fixation did have its down side. James recalls one day in the studio when Elvis became just a little too exuberant about the sport.

"Elvis loved it so much," he says. "He would put on little shows for us and show us what he'd learnt that day. I remember doing a session with him in Nashville at RCA's Studio B. Elvis would work awhile and we'd cut a few things and then take a break and send people out for food. Whilst that was going on Elvis was showing us some karate things he'd been working on. Things like how to take a gun away from someone if they'd pulled one on him. He had Red with him and said he was going to show the guys in the studio how it worked. He's talking away and the next thing the gun went flying right across the studio.

"Chip Young was there playing guitar with us. He had brought along a few guitars which I was using. One of his guitars was this incredible old Martin guitar. It was an amazing guitar, a masterpiece and certainly irreplaceable. Chips had these two guitars leaning against the wall and the gun flew across the room and hit one of the guitars. Chip, not even knowing which guitar it was that had been hit went 'oh no, man'. He just freaked out and put his hand over his face because he was afraid to look because he was worried that it was his favorite guitar. It ended up being the one I was playing that got hit, not the Martin. Chip was so relieved when he finally looked over at the wall. Elvis apologized and said 'oh sorry, man. I'll buy you a new guitar' and Chip said, 'don't worry about that one Elvis.' Elvis didn't mean to do it and probably bought Chip two or three guitars. And that didn't stop him doing the karate thing. He had this little guy who was around him all the time teaching him things and practicing with him where ever he went."

And certainly, there were times when the members of the T.C.B. Band who were actually into karate probably wished they hadn't taken up the sport. James recalls one night when Ronnie arrived for a show.

"He was black and blue," James says. "He and another guy called Dave, one of Elvis' bodyguards at the time and a guy who was very good at karate, had been sparing. This guy only had one eye, but he was incredible at karate. He and Ronnie got together and were sparing at a session and the result was that when we saw

Ronnie changing his shirt the next day before a show his body was black and blue with bruises. Ronnie actually got very upset by that. With karate you're actually not meant to make contact. You're supposed to come up real close but not actually connect with the other person's body, but this guy had hit Ronnie so many times he was really bruised."

There's absolutely no question that none of the T.C.B. Band had any sense of how these years of touring with Elvis would be regarded in the future. It was a lot more than just-another-gig for them but none of them realized how significant it would become in the history of rock'n'roll music.

"We had no idea," Ronnie smiles. "It's almost a thing where you'd better enjoy what you're doing because it may be around for a while if it's captured on tape or video. We didn't have a complete handle on, as you say, how important it was to so many people. Obviously, there were millions of fans around the world, but at the time we were almost unable to understand it and cope with it. There was, to be honest, a feeling of a little bit of embarrassment and yet at the same time the knowledge that it really was great."

CHAPTER 6

RECORDING WITH ELVIS

Chapter Six

Elvis recorded two albums at Graceland during the time the T.C.B. Band performed with him along with a number of studio albums and what seemed like endless live albums culled from concert performances with the T.C.B. Band.

At Graceland, a mobile unit was bought in for the recording with the studio being set up in the infamous Jungle Room

"It was kind of funny being there," Glen D recalls. "When we first went down there, we arrived on a Sunday night to record and as soon as we got there, we asked the people who worked there if they'd make us some coffee. This nice black lady said to me, 'no, I can't make no coffee. If I make some coffee it might wake up Mr. Elvis and we don't want to wake up Mr. Elvis.' So, we had to use the limousine and we'd keep the driver going out for coffee and pizza and fried chicken.

"It was funny. We always laughed that if you were the King of Rock'n'Roll you should be able to get us a cup of coffee at your own house. One time a few years ago I flew home from Switzerland with old D.J. Fontana. D.J. is really a fine old boy, a great guy. We got to talking and ended up talking all the way home. He told me that when he quit working with Elvis, Elvis told him that any time he was in Memphis he should come over to Graceland and drop in. D.J said, "But I didn't like to go over there, you couldn't even get a cup of coffee,' so we obviously weren't the first people to have trouble getting coffee at Graceland."

Elvis could be erratic during these recording sessions, probably in part because he had the luxury and security of being at home. The band would always stay at a hotel but be called to Graceland at around 6pm each day when the recording was scheduled.

Glen recalls one Sunday evening when they assembled at Graceland and there was no sign of Elvis. They were still kept at the studio till 5am the next morning just in case Elvis appeared and wanted to do some work. As it was, Elvis didn't appear until 4am the following Thursday morning.

"Now, we were getting paid, so we didn't care, but after a while you get tired of playing pool, watching TV and eating fried chicken. But that was the way it was. Elvis didn't show up until he was damned good and ready."

Jerry recalls that when he recorded at Graceland, Elvis wasn't in the best shape physically but that the sessions were still enjoyable.

"I wrote a song for Elvis and it's probably the most famous song that never got recorded," Jerry laughs. "We were going to record it at the studio at Graceland, but after about an hour Elvis said he wasn't feeling good and wanted to lie down. He went off to his bedroom, saying that he couldn't work then. He told the guys to go ahead and put the track down, but he never did do the vocal.

"Felton Jarvis' wife has said that Felton carried a tape of that track that we'd done around with him for two or three months afterwards, trying to get Elvis to do the vocal, but it never happened.

"The way the song happened was that we were on the Lisa Marie and Elvis was telling us that one of the reasons he bought the Lisa Marie was so that we could go overseas. I started talking to him and asked why he didn't do any of the new rock'n roll songs. Elvis said that he couldn't find any that he liked so I went home and premeditated this song called Island Of Love. I played it for Felton, and he said, 'if Elvis does that, it's a smash.' I signed the publishing rights away to them."

Whilst recording was being done at Graceland, things not surprisingly, became a little weird from time to time. Jerry recalls a time when Elvis decided to play dress-ups with the band.

"We were set up and ready to play and record. I don't remember exactly how this went down, but Charlie Hodge came over and put a note on my music stand saying 'Elvis wants to see you upstairs' so I walked up the stairs and knocked on the door and Elvis opened it. He was standing there in a Denver Police Captain's Uniform, the whole deal. He said, 'come on in Jerry' and I walked in and there's Denver Police Officers sitting on his bed and in chairs. It was a little Fellini-esque, a little bit surreal. So, I went in and Elvis introduced me. He said, 'come in here' and took me into his closet, which was the size of my living room. He looked at me then thumbed through a whole bunch of clothes - racks and racks of them - and there was this row of suits in different colors. They had fur cuffs on them, and matching hats with rhinestone belt buckles on the front. He pulled one of those off the rack and told me to try it on, so I agreed and went and tried it on. It was too big. I asked Elvis where he'd got it from and he said 'oh, I was walking down the street one day and I said ' look at those suits there' and Sonny and Red went in after I'd told them to get them all in this size'" but he said that he'd never wear them. They were kind of Superfly looking. So, he looked until he found a valet jacket and he tried that on me, and it fit real good so he sent me downstairs with that.

"Then Elvis started bringing other people upstairs and what I got from this was that he was planning to wear that Denver Policeman's Captain's uniform to record in - which he did - so he was going to dress everybody up. That was one of the fun sides of him. I love this story because that's the Elvis I like to remember. We hadn't sat around and drunk or taken drugs or anything else like that, we were just sitting there with the policemen.

"We got J. D. Sumner and the Stamps in the Superfly suits which fit them, then they came down and we proceeded to record. For a while, no one could keep a straight face but then we got serious. The sun was coming up and the LA people went in the Tristar and Elvis said, 'I've got to get J.D. and the Stamps back to Nashville . . . Charlie, go get the stretch limo.' So, Charlie went and got this big white Lincoln limousine and Elvis gave it to them: 'J.D., this is for you'. So, we went out on the porch of Graceland as the sun was coming up and here's J.D. Sumner and the Stamps in Superfly and we're waving goodbye and I've never laughed so hard, to see these guys sitting in this stretch white limo in those Superfly suits. That was hilarious. J.D. Sumner said they were on their way up to Nashville and they stopped at a McDonalds . . . they pulled up at the window to get some Egg McMuffins or whatever and J.D. said to the guy in the window who was checking them out - the limo and the suits - and when they left J.D. says that the guy looked at them and said 'you be cool . . . no, you're already cool'"

Recalling that moment, Jerry has reason to recall one of the most endearing aspects of working with Elvis - his sense of humor.

"Elvis was like a big kid in a lot of ways", he says. "He really was. I always got that impression. I'd heard about when he went to high school and was growing up and it seems like he was pretty much a loner a lot of the time when he was growing up. I think he had Sonny and all those guys that were around him, and this was like a complete counter thing to his high school days. It was like the male bonding thing he didn't have when he was in school."

It was during one recording session at Graceland that Jerry unwittingly became the rather public victim of a practical joke. Jerry had flown in from Los Angeles where he'd been working all day doing back-to-back sessions. He finished at about 6pm in the evening and caught one of the last flights of the night to Memphis. When he arrived, everyone else was set up and Elvis was ready to record, but Jerry was completely exhausted.

"David Briggs was in the studio and so I got my bass out and set up. Then I went over to David and asked him if he had any uppers with him because I was about to fall asleep on my feet. He said he did and put a pill in my hand. It was a Quaalude. He knew it, but obviously I didn't because otherwise I would never have taken it. David went over to Elvis and the guys and obviously said 'watch Jerry Scheff'. All of them had their eyes on me and, sure enough, right in the middle of the take, my hands turned to butter and just slid off the bass. Then they loaded me up with coffee. I don't think I'd ever taken a Quaalude until that time. It's a muscle relaxant and your limbs just feel like they're limp. I kept wondering why Elvis was watching me so much whilst I was playing. As it turned out, that was the take that was used on the album we were recording because I had to go and put the bass part on later."

Glen recalls that recording with Elvis was always relatively casual. "He always had a lot of singers around. Elvis was just great at working with singers. He could always tell them parts he wanted them to sing. With vocal groups he knew everybody's parts. They had the freedom to join in and do things on their own, but usually what Elvis suggested was the best. Sometimes recording would be real quick and other times we'd just go on and on at it so that it seemed like we'd been in the studio forever."

The majority of the recording sessions were however not at Graceland, but at the RCA Studios in Los Angeles.

"I'll tell you something funny," Glen says. "We recorded one time at RCA in Studio C. We recorded every night for a week, and from what I recall there were eight hits in the stuff we put down. I know we cut Burning Love and a bunch of other great songs at those sessions. A lot of artists, particularly when they have some hits, always want to be in that same studio for good luck, but the funny thing is that we never recorded there again so I guess Elvis wasn't very superstitious."

Elvis and the band, whilst usually happy with the way recording sessions went, weren't always delighted with the results they heard on vinyl. They'd experienced disappointment with the live recording from the Madison Square Garden concerts which had been sped up, in theory to enable more songs to be put on the album. But the same sometimes happened to studio recordings.

"I remember one time we recorded at Graceland and heard the finished album after it was pressed," Ronnie recalls. "It was a wonderful recording and yet when we got the final pressing it was a case of 'wait a minute, what's wrong with this thing?' We couldn't figure it out and then we found out that the whole thing had been sped up so that he (the Colonel) could get extra songs on it. By speeding it up it made Elvis' voice sound a little bit silly, and all the tempos were out. That was part of the stuff that was done behind Elvis' back, stuff that he didn't know.

"I do know that he got to a point when we were recording at Graceland once and he called us all up to his bedroom and played us a recording of somebody else. It was a rock group, but I can't remember their name. Basically, he was asking us, because he knew we had a lot of experience in the studio and were very much involved in the industry, why his records didn't sound anything like what he was playing to us by this other group. The whole thing goes back to the Colonel wanting his boy to be out there as seventy percent of the sound and the rhythm section way, way down at the bottom. The reason he often didn't sound supported and strong on records was because the Colonel wouldn't allow it. He'd take things and re-mix them without Elvis being told or involved."

CHAPTER 7

ELVIS HAS LEFT THE BUILDING…

Chapter Seven

Ronnie Tutt remembers being at home the day he heard the news that Elvis had died. He hadn't seen Elvis for a few months, having been busy playing and recording with Jerry Garcia.

"My mother-in-law called and said 'you're not going to believe that I've heard' so I immediately called Graceland and Felton Jarvis picked up the phone and I asked him if it was true and he told me that yes, Elvis had died. We talked briefly and he told me it was a zoo at Graceland and not to come out unless I felt I had to. I didn't want to make my association with Elvis seem more than what it was and use it for any publicity purposes. I just went out in my garden and said my little piece with him. It's weird to think about it now. There had been a drought in California for several months and the minute I had it confirmed that Elvis had died and went into my garden a little misty rain started coming down, so it was quite a moving time."

One of the things that the T.C.B. Band members are often asked and something they've discussed together many times over the years is whether or not they could - or should - have said or done anything to maybe help slow down or alter the decline they all witnessed in Elvis' health.

"I'm not sure any of us was in a position to do that," Ronnie says. "I believe he was a lot more ill than he let on - and that a lot of people realized. One night before he passed on, I came into the dressing room and he was telling me about some medical problems he had. I can't remember exactly what the terms were, but I was surprised to hear that he had pains in his abdominal area. I know he was having problems with his eyes. The lights and the flashbulbs were killing him. You'd go and see him before a show and his eyes would be closed and there'd be tears coming down his cheeks. I understand that. My eyes also became very light sensitive because I played right behind him, so I saw that sea of flashlights and bulbs every time he would come onstage. It was pretty amazing."

Glen was another band member who couldn't help but notice the disintegration in Elvis towards the end of his career.

"I left about a year and a half before he died because things had changed, and it wasn't as much fun. When he got into the drugs thing everything was different. I never actually saw Elvis take drugs and I never took drugs with him, but I know that he did because I could tell when he was flying high.

"When he started doing drugs, playing the shows got really uninteresting to me and he lost his focus. It was just very different. As a matter of fact, it came to the point where the set list didn't change anymore. We were just running through the same thing. I started getting tired of doing the same old show over and over and I really missed the improvisation.

"In November of '74 we did Emmylou's first album and then in 1975 James and I started working with her because she booked her entire schedule around Elvis' schedule so that she could have me and James. We got to the end of that year and I had worked way too hard. It was too much, and I knew that I had to make a decision and let one of them go. I decided that I wanted to stay with Emmy. That's partly because things were getting different with Elvis."

So how did Elvis take the news that Glen did wanted to leave the T.C.B. Band?

"Well, I never did talk to him," Glen says. "I called up Tom Diskin and told him that I'd come to a decision that I wouldn't be there on tour anymore and that I wanted him to tell Elvis that I'd really enjoyed working with him. I thought I might call Elvis myself, but I never did.

"Tom Diskin started saying 'well, you know you can't quit, I can't tell Elvis that.' And I said 'well, I'm going to quit, I've got something else and I want to move on.' He kept saying 'well, you can't do that, you can't quit Elvis, nobody quits Elvis.' I said, 'well, tell him I died or that I jumped off a cliff or something'. He kept saying that I couldn't quit and so finally I said to him 'when you guys are out there on tour and you look up there at the piano and you notice that I'm not there, I've not quit . . . I just won't be there.' He finally got it through his head. Mr. Diskin was a wonderful, nice man but he worked for the Colonel."

Looking back on the time with Elvis, James puts the emotions well when asked whether he ever had a sense that the time he played with the T.C.B. Band would be considered so historically important.

"I'd been playing with a lot of people by the time I heard from Elvis but getting the call from him was a complete thrill because Elvis was number one and I think anybody in the music business at any given time would have given their right arm to work with him. It was a great feeling to work with the King of Rock'n'Roll."

CHAPTER 8

“I CALLED A REHEARSAL, AND ALL THESE OLD GUYS WALKED IN…”

Chapter Eight

Joe remembers the first rehearsal for Elvis -The Concert being particularly emotional for everyone involved.

"Ronnie and I had been working together on tracks. We'd look at some of the footage such as I'll Remember You and there's Glen sitting back there and Jerry's out there with a beard and red hair, and The Sweet Inspirations are all sitting out front. I said to Ronnie that our first rehearsal was going to be something because some of us hadn't seen each other for so long. Everybody starts to walk in, and I said to Ronnie 'wow, look at all these old people'.

We got up there, and I swear to God that from the moment we started it was something special. We started with C.C. Rider and it was like we'd closed the night before when we last played together with Elvis. We're talking 22 years on and it still roared. We got to Steamroller Blues and the girls got chocked up and so emotional that we had to stop and take a 15 minute break. We came back after that break and we've been roaring ever since. It's like we just came out of that 15 minute break and it's 22 years later.

All of the T.C.B. Band agree that if it wasn't for Stig Edgren's involvement, Elvis - The Concert would never have happened, certainly on the scale it has.

"Someone called and offered me $1000 for one show," Joe laughs. "That wasn't going to work. That didn't make any sense. I didn't even return the phone call. Then Stig came in and organized it. He got everyone on the phone. I knew Stig because he did a lot of shows in Las Vegas. Stig originally was a lighting director, a really good one. He knows how that side of a show works as well as anyone."

Glen was certainly reluctant to be involved when first contacted about the project.

“I don’t know exactly why I felt that way,” he says, midway through the Australian tour. “When they called me and explained the concept I said, ‘I think it’s the worst idea I’ve ever heard, and I don’t think it’ll work.’ I just had no idea how good it could be I guess, but I did tell them that if the other boys wanted to do it, I certainly wanted to be in it. I would never shoot it down if everyone else thought it was a good idea. So, we went down to Memphis to put it together for them. We knew it was going to take some work. Then Ronnie got to wondering about the tapes and what we would actually get to hear. He called someone at Graceland and got copies. They had no idea. They thought we could just sit down and look at the pictures and go ‘oh yeah, I know that song, let’s have a go at it.’

“As it happened Ronnie and Joe took the tapes into the studio. Ronnie put on a lot of clicks and things that we could hear and use to keep time. Even so, there’s a lot of places where we get started with a song and the click goes away and we’re just following Elvis’ vocal because he’s so on top of it. Then there’ll be places where we’ll come back in where we know exactly where we are. It’s not easy to do, that’s for sure. We’ve really got to pay attention because if you miss your cue, you’re just plain out of luck. It’s like a train leaving a station - it’s going to leave with you, or without you.”

APPENDIX ONE

THE VOCAL GROUPS

J.D. SUMNER & THE STAMPS

The lowest vocal bass note ever recorded by the Guinness Book Of World Records came from J.D. Sumner. It's one of a long list of great moments in the life of a musical legend. For much of his career he headed up the Stamps Quartet, one of the greatest success stories in the gospel music industry. The group was nominated for Grammy, Dove and TNN awards, and toured the world in concert. Sumner is credited with being a major force in the formation of the Gospel Music Association, the Dove Awards and the National Quartet Convention, and for being a significant influence in leading the gospel world to even greater levels of professionalism and organization. His direction and management of the Stamps was a model for many other groups. The Stamps worked with Elvis Presley from 1971 to 1977 as the male back-up group for his concerts in Las Vegas and on national tour, and they worked with him on numerous recordings. J.D. Sumner (bass), Ed Enoch (lead) and Ed Hill (baritone), the latter singing with the Stamps in the last two years of the period, were joined at various times by Bill Baize, Donnie Sumner, Larry Strickland, and current Oak ridge Boys member Richard Sterban. J.D. Sumner died in 1998.

THE IMPERIALS

Elvis loved gospel music, particularly male gospel harmony, which was not only a major part of his gospel recordings, but also an element in the sound of so much of his pop, rock and country work. The Imperials first worked with Elvis doing some of the great backing vocals in the 1966 sessions for his How Great Thou Art album, which won Elvis his first Grammy Award, Best Sacred

Performance for 1967. The Imperials worked on a regular basis with Elvis on stage and in the recording studio from 1969 until the latter half of 1971, beginning with the triumphant Las Vegas engagement. A major highlight of their collaboration with him was the 1971 records (1972 release) of He Touched Me, an album that earned Elvis his second Grammy award, Best Inspirational Performance for 1972. Gospel legend and former Statesmen Quartet member Jake Hess founded the Imperials in 1964, putting together what he would call a "super group" in the gospel music industry. By the late '60s, they had a new look and sound, a bit on the "mod" side, which drew criticism from some circles, but the group prevailed. They sold a lot of records, enjoyed a long series of major TV guest spots, toured with country singer Jimmy Dean and appeared regularly on his weekly TV show, and the group had regular bookings in Las Vegas, Reno and Lake Tahoe. And, of course, there was the special association with Elvis Presley. Over the years, the group in its various membership incarnations has released over forty albums with fourteen of their songs hitting number one, and they have racked up twelve Grammy Awards and thirteen of the gospel field's Dove Awards. They were the first Christian group to perform on a Grammy Awards telecast. Their catalogue of songs is one of the most enduring in all of gospel music, many of them landmark recordings that raised the standards for the gospel music industry at large. Like Elvis' other male back-up groups, The Jordanaires and The Stamps, The Imperials', current and former members are recent inductees into the Gospel Music association's Hall of Fame – the members included; Armond Morales, Jim Murray, Joe Moscheo, Terry Blackwood, and Sherman Andrus.

THE SWEET INSPIRATIONS

The soulful harmonies of the Sweet Inspirations have enriched recordings by Aretha Franklin, Wilson Pickett and other legends. They have collaborated with writers and producers such as Carol

King, Burt Bacharach and Hal David. They've had success with R&B, gospel and pop recordings of their own, most notably their first hit single Sweet Inspiration, which gave the group their name in the late '60s and earned them a Grammy nomination. It was that song that caught the attention of Elvis Presley, who signed them to provide backing vocals and be an opening act for his record-breaking 1969 Las Vegas engagement, his official return to the live concert stage after his triumphant '69 TV special and the end of his Hollywood movie contract obligations. No audition was required. The Sweet Inspirations met him when they arrived for the first rehearsals for the '69 engagement. The "Sweets" worked with Elvis in Vegas, on his national concert tours and on recordings from 1969 to 1977. Myrna Smith, Sylvia Shemwell, Estelle Brown and Cissy Houston (mother of superstar Whitney) made up the original group. Houston left the group to go solo after the first gig with Elvis. Smith, Shemwell and Brown stayed together through the Elvis years, but eventually went their separate ways professionally. In the nineties, the three reunited as a group and have been performing and recording together again, and they have re-established the Elvis connection with various projects with Graceland. In the mid-1990's, Portia Griffin joined the group, and later, Kelley Jones. Myrna Smith recalls that first meeting with Elvis. "He walked in and had on a chocolate colored suit. He had a tan, and he looked absolutely gorgeous. He walked over to us and introduced himself - like we didn't know who he was: 'Hi, I'm Elvis Presley.' (Cissy literally fell off her stool.) From then on, whenever he'd see us, it was always a kiss." Smith remembers his talent - "He had so much energy. His voice was a lot more remarkable than it ever came off on record . . . He was just a much better singer than could ever be captured . . . Some great singers' voices are just too big. Elvis' was like that."

APPENDIX TWO

OTHER MUSICIANS WHO APPEARED WITH ELVIS

JOHN WILKINSON

John Wilkinson played rhythm guitar with the T.C.B. Band.

CHARLIE HODGE

Charlie Hodge, who was nicknamed Slewfoot and Waterhead) met Elvis back in 1956. He was a singer, guitarist and assistant to Elvis, living in a converted apartment behind Graceland for seventeen years. Only five feet three inches tall, Hodge was one of the shortest members of the Memphis Mafia and to compensate wore lifts in his shoes. He was stationed with Elvis in West Germany. Hodge and Elvis recorded a duet of I Will Be Home Again in 1960. It was Hodge's responsibility to look after Elvis personal life and music schedule. He was the person who drove Priscilla and Elvis to the hospital on the day that Lisa Marie was born. It was been suggested that Hodge witnessed Elvis' will. He, with Red West and Elvis, wrote You'll Be Gone. He had cameo parts in the films Charro! And Clambake and appeared as himself in Elvis in 1979, and was a feature character in the 1988 TV drama Elvis And Me. Through the 70s he performed with the T.C.B. Band.

DUKE BARDWELL

Bass player who worked with Elvis in the studio and on stage in the mid-70s

HAL BLAINE

Hal Blaine at times played drums with the T.C.B. Band.

TONY BROWN

Tony Brown was the piano player who replaced Glen D. Hardin in the T.C.B. Band during 1974 - 77.

MARTY HARRELL

Marty Harrell played trombone with the T.C.B. Band.

PAT HOUSTON

Pat Houston played trumpet with the T.C.B. Band

LARRY MAHOBEREC

Keyboard player who preceded Glen Hardin, and also recommended Ron Tutt for the gig.

JIMMY MULIDORE

Jimmy Mulidore played the flute solo during the February 17, 1972 live recording of American Trilogy from Las Vegas.

JOE OSBORNE

Joe Osborne on occasions played bass with the T.C.B. Band.

JERRY SHOOK

Jerry Shook played bass in the T.C.B. Band when Jerry Scheff was not available.

APPENDIX THREE

ELVIS PRESLEY - PIVOTAL LIVE MOMENTS - 1969-1977

Information from The Ultimate Elvis - Patricia Jobe Pierce

1969

JULY 1 - Colonel Parker travels to Las Vegas to finalize planning for Elvis' season in Las Vegas, distributing over 6,000 posters in the city and placing full-page advertisements in all major newspapers.

JULY 20 - Elvis arrives in Las Vegas and is mobbed by hundreds of fans. This is also the day Neil Armstrong became the first man to step foot on the moon.

JULY 24 - Marquees announce the upcoming Elvis shows.

JULY 27 - Elvis and the musicians rehearse in Las Vegas. It is the first time Priscilla sees Elvis perform.

JULY 27 - 29 - More than five thousand telegrams arrive for Elvis from around the globe. Those attending the dress rehearsals include Dionne Warwick, Dick Clark, Carol Channing, Ed Ames, Paul Anka, Angie Dickinson, Burt Bacharach, Pat Boone, Fats Domino, Ann-Margaret, George Hamilton, Henry Mancini, Sam Phillips, Liberace and Wayne Newton. It has been said that Tom Jones felt jealous of Elvis popularity in Las Vegas (even though they had become friends) and remained in his hotel room.

JULY 31 - Opening night at the International Hotel. Liberace and Herb Alpert are in the audience, the first of 1, 126 shows over the next eight years. In recognition of man's first steps on the moon, the Sweet Inspirations begin the show with How High The Moon. Income from the shows were more than $1.5 million - and that was just from ticket sales.

AUGUST 1 - Elvis told newspaper reporters in Las Vegas that he was planning a world tour. The Colonel was not impressed. Neither was Priscilla who returned to Memphis when told that if the tour went ahead, she would have to stay home and look after the baby.

AUGUST 2 - Elvis was awarded a gold belt at the Las Vegas International Hotel in recognition of achieving "the world's championship attendance record."

AUGUST 11 - Newsweek reviewed a performance and stated that, "The pasty-faced enchanter quickly settled back to work his oleaginous charms, backed by a thirty-piece orchestra, a five-man combo, and a chorus of seven . . . Oozing the sullen sexuality that threw America into a state of shock in the fifties, he groaned and swiveled . . . (and) it was hard to believe he was thirty-four and no longer nineteen years old.".

AUGUST 22 - John Wayne's son Patrick was introduced onstage by Elvis

AUGUST 24 - A performance of Elvis singing My Babe by Willie Dixon and Charles Stone was recorded at the International Hotel. The concert that night can be heard on a variety of live albums, including Elvis Aaron Presley (Las Vegas, August 1969).

AUGUST 25 - Elvis performs Lennon and McCartney's Yesterday in a medley with the Beatles' Hey Jude.

AUGUST 26 - Elvis recorded Tiger Man which can be heard on the album Elvis In Person.

AUGUST 28 - After an exhausting run of shows a tired Elvis concludes his first season at the International Hotel in Las Vegas.

NOVEMBER 16 - From Memphis To Vegas/ From Vegas To Memphis was released. The first two sides of the double album were culled from performances at the International Hotel in August.

NOVEMBER - After seven years without a number 1 record, Elvis is back on the top of the charts with Suspicious Minds.

1970

JANUARY 22 - Elvis and the T.C.B. Band rehearse for a second season at the International Hotel in Las Vegas. Fifty-seven shows are scheduled between January 26 and February 23.

JANUARY 26 - Dean Martin was in the audience at the first night of the new season at the International Hotel. To mark the occasion Elvis sang Everybody Loves Somebody.

FEBRUARY 17 - The Las Vegas concert is recorded with performances featured on the albums Elvis - A Legendary Performer; Vol 3 and On Stage - February 1970.

FEBRUARY 23 - Elvis' last performance at the International Hotel in Las Vegas.

FEBRUARY 27 - MARCH 1 - Elvis breaks all previous records by singing to 207,494 fans over the course of six shows at the Houston Astrodome during the Texas Livestock Show.

AUGUST 10 - Elvis began another fifty-eight show season at the International Hotel in Las Vegas.

SEPTEMBER 7 - The International Hotel season concludes.

NOVEMBER 11 - Elvis performed at the Memorial Coliseum in Portland, Oregon on what was named Elvis Presley Day.

1971

JANUARY 26 - Elvis began another season of fifty-seven shows in Las Vegas. Whenever possible Elvis visited other performers headlining in Las Vegas at the time, including Liberace and Tom Jones.

JULY 20 - AUGUST 2 - Elvis performed twenty-eight shows in Stateline, Nevada at the Sahara Tahoe.

AUGUST 1 - Paul Anka attends a concert at the Sahara.

AUGUST 9 - SEPTEMBER 6 - Elvis performed fifty-seven concerts at the Hilton Hotel in Las Vegas.

DECEMBER 23 - Rolling Stone, America's premier rock music magazine, wrote: "The magnificence of Presley's performance lies in its presentation of his as royalty. He is the one entertainer in the world who doesn't have to take out any insurance on his fame, success, grandeur, or greatness. He is the one and only performer who can simply revel in it and us with him."

1972

JANUARY 26 - FEBRUARY 23 - Elvis gave fifty-seven performances at the Las Vegas Hilton. As usual all were sold out.

APRIL 5 - Elvis appeared in Buffalo, New York at the Memorial Auditorium. The opening of this concert was captured on film for Elvis On Tour. Parts of each concert from now until April 19 were filmed. When completed Elvis On Tour was seen at 187 cinemas in 105 cities and grossed $494,270 in just one week.

JUNE 1 - 5 - Elvis and the T.C.B. Band rehearsed for their four sold-out shows at Madison Square Garden in New York.

DATES - Elvis performs possibly the finest shows of his career at Madison Square Garden.

AUGUST 4 - SEPTEMBER 4 - Elvis performs another sixty-three shows at the Hilton Hotel in Las Vegas. He is visited backstage a number of times by Sammy Davis, Jnr.

AUGUST 30 - At a benefit concert at Madison Square Garden in New York John Lennon yelled out “I love you, Elvis.”

1973

JANUARY 9 - Elvis flew by helicopter to the Hawaiian Village Hotel in Honolulu.

JANUARY 10 - 11 - Elvis puts himself, the T.C.B. Band and other performers through exhausting rehearsals for the TV show Elvis; Aloha From Hawaii.

JANUARY 12 - Six thousand fans watch the dress rehearsals at the Honolulu International Center Arena.

JANUARY 13 - Honolulu, Hawaii declares it to be Elvis Presley Day.

JANUARY 14 - Elvis: Aloha From Hawaii was beamed worldwide by an Intelsat 1V communications satellite to approximately one billion people in forty countries at 12.30am (Honolulu time). The production cost $2.5 million. According to figures later released ninety-two percent of the TV audience in the Philippines watched the show. It was also the first time fans in China, Japan, South

Korea, New Zealand, South Vietnam, Thailand, the Far East and Australia could see Elvis perform.

JANUARY 15 - Elvis: Aloha From Hawaii was rebroadcast and shown in twenty-eight European countries.

JANUARY 26 - Elvis and his musicians began a fifty-four show season at the Las Vegas Hilton. Elvis was forced to cancel three shows during to fatigue.

MAY 4 - 16 - Although scheduled to play twenty-five shows in Stateline, Nevada at the Sahara Tahoe Hotel, Elvis had to cancel some performances due to exhaustion, stomach cramps and severe headaches.

MAY 7 - George Harrison visited Elvis. The former Beatle and Elvis kept in regular contact after this.

AUGUST 6 - After extensive touring an exhausted Elvis began a run of fifty-nine concerts at the Hilton Hotel in Las Vegas.

SEPTEMBER 3 - The Hilton season concluded, with Elvis cancelling only two shows as a result of illness.

1974

JANUARY 24 -Whilst rehearsing for yet another Las Vegas season Elvis knelt down in the audience and sang part of The Most Beautiful Girl to comedian Marty Allen.

JANUARY 26 - Elvis began the twenty-six show season at the Las Vegas Hilton. All shows were sold out weeks prior and it has been reported that scalpers were getting $500 for a ticket - one that had cost $35 when originally put on sale.

MARCH 12 - Traditionally Elvis' concerts were relatively short, but it has been reported at this show at the Coliseum in Richmond, Virginia, he performed for almost three hours.

MAY 16 - After extensive touring around the United States Elvis returned to the Sahara Tahoe Hotel in Nevada for another twenty-six show season. The series of concerts ended on May 26.

AUGUST 15 - Elvis and his entourage travelled to Las Vegas to prepare for another season of shows.

AUGUST 19 - Barbra Streisand visited Elvis at the Hilton Hotel to discuss the idea of him co-starring with her in the film A Star Is Born. The role later went to Kris Kristofferson.

AUGUST 19 - SEPTEMBER 2 - Although extremely tired Elvis managed to perform twenty-seven of the twenty-nine shows scheduled at the Hilton Hotel in Las Vegas.

OCTOBER 1 - Elvis performed at the Notre Dame Athletic & Convention Center in South Bend, Indiana. He was allowed to use Playboy magazine publisher Hugh Hefner's black DC-9 jet to fly to and from the shows.

OCTOBER 11 - 14 - Elvis performed eight shows at the Sahara Tahoe Hotel in Nevada. The shows were, naturally, sold out - but Elvis looked increasingly tired.

1975

MARCH 14 - Elvis and his musicians travelled to Las Vegas to rehearse for another season at the Hilton Hotel.

MARCH 18 - The first of twenty-nine shows scheduled at the Hilton Hotel.

APRIL 25 - Fans became upset when Elvis gave an extremely short performance at the Veteran's Memorial Coliseum in Jacksonville, Florida. The reason was that Elvis was extremely ill and unable to continue the performance.

MAY 5 - A show at the State Fair Coliseum was a benefit for victims of a hurricane in McComb, Mississippi and raised $108,000.

MAY 28 - Bruce Springsteen was in the audience for a show at the Philadelphia Spectrum.

JULY 19 - Uncharacteristically Elvis played piano at a concert at Nassau Coliseum in Uniondale, New York, singing You'll Never Walk Alone.

JULY 20 - Elvis insulted Kathy Westmoreland and two of the Sweet Inspirations during a concert in Norfolk, Virginia. Myrna Smith remained onstage but refused to accept a ring (by way of an apology) offered by Elvis. He later apologized to the singers and gave each of them a ring valued at $5,000.

AUGUST 18 - 20 - Although Elvis was scheduled to perform for three weeks at the Las Vegas Hilton he cancelled the majority due to illness. During one of the concerts that did go ahead he sang Happy Birthday to You to James Burton.

DECEMBER 2 - Elvis returned to Las Vegas for seventeen shows at the Hilton Hotel.

DECEMBER 15 - The Las Vegas season ended, the final show being highlighted by a half hour rendition of gospel songs and other Elvis favorites.

DECEMBER 31 - Elvis performed on New Year's Eve at Pontiac, Michigan, the show breaking concert receipt records with a gross of $816,000 paid by 62,500 fans. During the concert Elvis accidentally split his pants, the Sweet Inspirations moving to center stage to sing Sweet, Sweet Spirit whilst the problem was rectified.

1976

APRIL 30 - After many, many concerts and recording sessions Elvis began a fifteen show stand at the Sahara Tahoe Hotel in Nevada.

MAY 6 - Elvis invited impressionist Douglas Roy to join him onstage.

JULY 5 - Such was the demand for tickets for a concert at the Mid-South Coliseum in Memphis that there was almost a riot. Police were called to patrol the streets and backstage areas.

DECEMBER 2 - After more grueling touring Elvis began a season at the Las Vegas Hilton. It would be the last times he performed in the city.

DECEMBER 12 - The final performance of the fifteen show stint at the Hilton in Las Vegas. The show ended with Elvis singing Suspicious Minds, My way and The American Trilogy.

1977

FEBRUARY 20 - Elvis introduced girlfriend Linda Thompson onstage at the Coliseum in Charlotte, North Carolina. She performed a classical piano number - one that didn't go down a storm with the audience.

JUNE 19 - Elvis In Concert was filmed by CBS-TV at the Omaha Civic Auditorium in Omaha, Nebraska.

JUNE 26 - Elvis performed for the last time at the Market Square Arena in Indianapolis, Indiana. At this stage he had completed fifty six concerts that year. Elvis and several band members became ill whilst in Indianapolis and were forced to spend a night in hospital.

APPENDIX FOUR

QUOTES ABOUT ELVIS PRESLEY

"Without preamble, the three-piece band cuts loose. In the spotlight, the lanky singer flails furious rhythms on his guitar. Every now and then breaking a string. In a pivoting stance, his hips swing sensuously from side to side and his entire body takes on a frantic quiver, as if he had swallowed a jack-hammer."
Time Magazine, 1956

"It isn't enough to say that Elvis is kind to his parents, sends money home, and is the same unspoiled kid he was before all the commotion began. That still isn't a free ticket to behave like a sex maniac in public."
Eddie Condon, Cosmopolitan Magazine, 1956

"I wanted to say to Elvis Presley and the country that this is a real decent, fine boy."
Ed Sullivan, 1957

"There are several unbelievable things about Elvis, but the most incredible is his staying power in a world where meteoric careers fade like shooting stars."
Newsweek, 1969

". . . a style and panache that come close to pure magic. Lithe, raunchy, the sweat pouring down his face, he now moves with the precision of an athlete, the grace of a dancer . . . flamboyant and flashy, sexy and self-mocking, he works with the instincts of a genius to give poetry to the basic rock performance."
Author W.A. Harbinson, recalling Elvis of 1969

"A lot of people have accused Elvis of stealing the black man's music, when in fact, almost every black solo entertainer copied his stage mannerisms from Elvis."
Jackie Wilson

"You have no idea how great he is, really you don't. You have no comprehension - it's absolutely impossible. I can't tell you why he's so great, but he is. He's sensational."
Phil Spector

"Elvis is the greatest cultural force in the twentieth century. He introduced the beat to everything, music, language, clothes, it's a whole new social revolution - the 60's come from it."
Leonard Bernstein

"Elvis had an influence on everybody with his musical approach. He broke the ice for all of us."
Al Green

". . . At Sun Studio in Memphis Elvis Presley called to life what would soon become known as rock and roll with a voice that bore strains of the Grand Ole Opry and Beale Street, of country and the blues. At that moment, he ensured - instinctively, unknowingly - that pop music would never again be as simple as black and white."
David Fricke, Rolling Stone Magazine

"There have been a lotta tough guys. There have been pretenders. There have been contenders. But there is only one king."
Bruce Springsteen
"When I first heard Elvis' voice I just knew that I wasn't going to work for anybody; and nobody was going to be my boss . . . Hearing him for the first time was like busting out of jail."
Bob Dylan

"Elvis was the king. No doubt about it. People like myself and all the others only followed in his footsteps."
Rod Stewart

"He was a unique artist - an original in an area of imitators."
Mick Jagger

"Before Elvis, there was nothing."
John Lennon

"This boy had everything. He had the looks, the moves, the manager, and the talent. And he didn't look like Mr. Ed like a lot of the rest of us did. In the way he looked, way he talked, way he acted - he really was different."
Carl Perkins

"I wasn't just a fan, I was his brother. He said I was good, and I said he was good; we never argued about that. Elvis was a hard worker, dedicated, and God loved him. Last time I saw him was at Graceland. We sang Old Blind Barnabus together, a gospel song. I love him and hope to see him in heaven. There'll never be another like that soul brother."
James Brown

"That's my idol, Elvis Presley. If you went to my house, you'd see pictures all over of Elvis. He's just the greatest entertainer that ever lived. And I think it's because he had such presence. When Elvis walked into a room, Elvis Presley was in the fucking room. I don't give a fuck who was in the room with him, Bogart, Marilyn Monroe."
Eddie Murphy

'It's rare when an artist's talent can touch an entire generation of people. It's even rarer when that same influence affects several generations. Elvis made an imprint on the world of pop music unequalled by any other single performer."
Dick Clark

". . . if any individual of our time can be said to have changed the world, Elvis Presley is the one. In his wake more than music is different. Nothing and no one looks or sounds the same. His music was the most liberating event of our era because it taught us new possibilities of feeling and perception, new modes of action and appearance, and because it reminded us not only of his greatness, but of our own potential."
Music Writer, Greil Marcus

"Elvis Presley was an explorer of vast new landscapes of dream and illusion. He was a man who refused to be told that the best of his dreams would not come true, who refused to be defined by anyone else's perceptions. This is the goal of democracy, the journey on which every American hero sets out. That Elvis made so much of the journey on his own is reason enough to remember him with the honor and love we reserve for the bravest among us. Such men made the only maps we can trust."
MusicWriter, Dave Marsh

"You know, Bush is always comparing me to Elvis in sort of unflattering ways. I don't think Bush would have liked Elvis very much, and that's just another thing that's wrong with him."
Bill Clinton, 1992

"He had total love in his eyes when he performed. He was the total androgynous beauty. I would practice Elvis in front of the mirror when I was twelve or thirteen years old."
k.d. lang

"He was the firstest with the mostest."
Roy Orbison

"I'm sitting in the drive-through and I've got my three girls in the back and this station comes on and it's playing Jailhouse Rock, the original version. And my girls are jumping up and down, going nuts. I'm looking around at them and they've heard Dad's music all the time and I don't see that out of them."
Garth Brooks

"Ask anyone. If it hadn't been for Elvis, I don't know where popular music would be. He was the one that started it all off, and he was definitely the start of it for me."
Elton John

"The first concert I attended was an Elvis concert when I was eleven. Even at that age he made me realize the tremendous effect a performer could have on an audience."
Cher

"Elvis was a giant and influenced everyone in the business."
Isaac Hayes

"I learned music listening to Elvis' records. His measurable effect on culture and music was even greater in England than in the States."
Mick Fleetwood

"I remember Elvis as a young man hanging around the Sun studios. Even then, I knew this kid had a tremendous talent. He was a dynamic young boy. His phraseology, his way of looking at a song, was as unique as Sinatra's. I was a tremendous fan, and had Elvis lived, there would have been no end to his inventiveness."
B.B. King

DISCOGRAPHY

Let's cut to the chase here. You don't need to hear every Elvis album released. It might shock some fans but there really is other music to listen to during your lifetime. For anyone bar the most obsessive fan - who, let's face it, will already own every album and single - here's some recommendations of music to hear from the period 1969 - 1977. The majority of it features the members of the T.C.B. Band.

Given the genesis of this book it's hard to go past the double CD on which Elvis - The Concert is based. The tracks, culled from various performances, are all from concerts and feature The T.C.B. Band.

Introduction: also, Sprach Zarathustra (theme from 2001: A Space Odyssey)
See See Rider
Burning Love
Steamroller Blues
I Can't Stop Loving You
Johnny B. Goode
You Gave Me A Mountain
Polk, Salad Annie
You've Lost That Loving Feeling
Proud Mary
Never Been To Spain
Just Pretend
Make The World Go Away
In The Ghetto
How Great Thou Art
Bridge Over Troubled Water

Trouble/ Guitar Man
Hound Dog
(Let Me Be Your) Teddy Bear/ Don't Be Cruel
All Shook Up
Heartbreak Hotel
One Night
Love Me Tender
The Wonder Of You
Lawdy Miss Clawdy
Funny How Time Slips Away
Suspicious Minds
I'll Remember You
A Big Hunk O'Love
My Way
An American Trilogy
Can't Help Falling In Love
Closing Vamp

BIBLIOGRAPHY

There are dozens and dozens of books about Elvis and I guess I've read most of them over the years. The following are books that shaped my understanding and appreciation of Elvis, particularly the period from 1969 - 1977. Some are obviously only about Elvis; others contain sections that for their Elvis content alone are worth the price of admission. Of these books a number are inspiring, the majority useful, and a handful, well . . .

Careless Love: The Unmaking of Elvis Presley by Peter Guralnick
Little, Brown, 1999

The Ultimate Elvis by Patricia Jobe Pierce
Simon & Schuster, 1994

Elvis by Dave Marsh
1982

Elvis: The Boy Who Dared To Rock by Paul Lichter
Sphere Books, 1980

I Called Him Babe: Elvis Presley's Nurse Remembers by Marian J. Cocke
Memphis State University Press, 1979

Down At The End Of Lonely Street: The Life And Death Of Elvis Presley by Peter Brown & Pat Broeske
Heinemann Books, 1997

Elvis by Jerry Hopkins
St Martin's Press, 1971

Elvis: The final Years by Jerry Hopkins
Star Books, 1981

Mystery Train: Images Of America In Rock'n'Roll by Greil Marcus
Plume Books, 1990

Elvis And The Colonel by Dirk Vellenga with Mick Farren
Grafton Books, 1989

Psychotic Reactions And Carburetor Dung by Lester Bangs
Knopf, 1987

AUTHOR ACKNOWLEDGMENTS

For providing me with three of the most enjoyable (and tiring) weeks of my life I'd like to thank Stig Edgren, James Burton, Ronnie Tutt, Jerry Scheff, Glen D. Hardin and Joe Guercio. Also, mucho thanks to the members of the Sweet Inspirations, The Imperials, Kelley Johnson, Carmen Rodriguez, Donna Tutt, Louise Burton and all members of the Elvis - The Concert crew.

Many laughs were also had with Mark Marriott, the superlative Australian drummer who joined the T.C.B. Band for the tour. And to publicist Robbie Harris for getting everything rolling in the first place and then making sure things stayed on track. Tour manager Wayne Jarvis made things one hell of a lot easier than they might otherwise have been and without promoter Kevin Jacobsen there wouldn't have been an Australian tour of Elvis - The Concert in the first place.

www.ingramcontent.com/pod-product-compliance
Lightning Source LLC
LaVergne TN
LVHW051006080826
845145LV00009B/2477

* 9 7 8 0 5 7 8 7 7 7 4 6 7 *